# LONGINGS

OF THE

# SOUL

THE HOLY SPIRIT AT WORK IN YOU

# LONGINGS

## OF THE

# SOUL

DISCOVER WHAT YOU ARE
REALLY LONGING FOR

## ROB SALVATO

**CALVARY VISTA**
*Simply Jesus*

LONGINGS OF THE SOUL
*Discover What You Are Really Longing For*

Copyright ©2017 by Rob Salvato

Published by Calvary Vista
885 E. Vista Way
Vista, California 92084

First printing, 2017

Cover and internal layout and design by Shahn Flood
Editing by Denise Salvato and Romy Godding

ISBN: 978-1-5408-9664-3

Printed in the United States of America

# CONTENTS

# ACKNOWLEDGMENTS

*To my best friend and wife, Denise*—thank you for inspiring me in my love for Jesus. Your love, support, and willingness to join me on this adventure we call life puts a smile on my face every day. Thank you for your tireless work of editing this book and the many other ways you assist me in serving Jesus!

*To the Calvary Vista church family*—I am so blessed to be a part of such an amazing group of people. I am privileged to serve as your pastor. I learn so much about the heart of our Savior from all of you.

*To Romy Godding, my copy editor*—thank you for being a faithful friend and an honest critic. You are a gifted editor and a joy to work with.

*To Shahn Flood*—thank you for capturing the heart of this book in your cover design. You are awesome, and your graphic skills are second to none!

*To Ron and Jacque Entzminger*—thank you for blessing me with the use of your vacation home and enabling me to get away to finish writing.

*To Amanda Sanford, my princess*—thank you for the cover photo.

*To Scott Sanford*—thanks for being the book cover image and a great son-in-law. Both of your hearts, talents, and lives bring me great joy!

# INTRODUCTION

When I was a kid growing up, there was a TV show that our family used to watch on a regular basis called *Candid Camera*. (This was before YouTube and *America's Funniest Home Videos*.) The show had hidden cameras filming ordinary people being confronted with unusual situations, sometimes involving trick props, such as a desk with drawers that pop open when one is closed or a car with a hidden extra gas tank. When the joke was revealed, victims would then hear the show's catchphrase, "Smile, you're on *Candid Camera*."

I will always remember the episode where an actor is walking in circles on a busy city sidewalk while intently staring at the ground, making it look like he is trying to find a lost object. The whole time, people are just passing by, most of them ignoring him, while a few give him some strange looks.

After a couple of minutes of this, the man decides to get down on his hands and knees and feel around on the sidewalk. Now people are slowing down to watch what he is doing. Finally, one person stops and starts looking on the ground as well, and then another; and pretty soon, there are a dozen or so people who have stopped and are staring at the ground. A few have even gone down on their hands and knees as well, feeling around, searching. At that point, the actor who had started the entire thing, slowly gets up and walks away, and no one notices that he has left because the people are so intent on their search. However, no one had bothered to ask what they were supposed to be searching for.

I believe that is a good picture of how many people are living their lives today. They are intently searching for something. They sense a longing in their hearts for something else, something more, something better. But they don't know what it is they are searching or longing for. So life becomes this proverbial quest for that which is going to bring purpose, satisfaction, and lasting fulfillment. And this is not just the plight of the person who has yet to come into a relationship with Jesus.

One of the great paradoxes of the Christian life is how Jesus can fill our hearts with peace because we've been forgiven—our guilt is removed, and we begin to enjoy the blessings of salvation—yet we can still struggle with feelings of discontentment, dissatisfaction, and discouragement. Our hearts are restless, but we don't know why! Our problem is very similar to what the people were doing on the sidewalk that day—we don't know what we are searching for. My heart for this book is to help believers in Jesus discover what it is we are really longing for.

*Longings of the Soul* is not about the plague of consumerism, because the issue is much deeper than that. Rather, it is about three distinct longings that have been placed in the heart of every believer in Jesus Christ because of the presence of God's Spirit in our lives. His very Spirit in our hearts is constantly nudging us in these three directions, toward three pursuits. These longings, which are spiritual in nature, are inherently at the center of all the others we wrestle with. And if we understand these longings and how to satisfy them, they will serve as sort of a "true north" in our lives and help us to navigate through the inner struggles we all experience. Once we recognize why and how the Holy Spirit is pulling us in these three directions, I believe our lives will take on an entirely new meaning and purpose, as we follow Jesus in this fallen world.

# LONGINGS OF THE SOUL

*"Oh, that men would give thanks to the LORD for His goodness, and for His wonderful works to the children of men! For He satisfies the longing soul, and fills the hungry soul with goodness."*

PSALM 107:8-9

"Satisfaction" by the Rolling Stones is one of rock music's definitive songs. It was the Stones first number one single on U.S. charts and would become their signature song. "(I Can't Get No) Satisfaction" was number one on Billboard's top 100 chart for four consecutive weeks and currently sits at number two on *Rolling Stone* magazine's list of greatest rock songs of all time. It is a song that continues to strike a nerve, from generation to generation, in people who identify with the frustration of feeling dissatisfied with life. The song vividly describes the problem, as Mick Jagger cries,

> 'Cause I try and I try and I try and I try
> I can't get no, I can't get no
> (June 1965, Out of Our Heads)

At some point in life, every human being who has ever lived has been on the losing end of that struggle, endlessly moving from one person, pleasure, or pursuit to another, hoping to find something that will satisfy the longing in his or her heart. We have all experienced being in a place where we thought, *This is it! The search is over!* only to find that the satisfaction we experienced with whatever the "it" was didn't last. So the search continued for another "it" experience to appease the longing in our hearts.

Oftentimes, we resemble the little child trying to fit the right plastic-shaped object into the right hole of their toy. I remember one day watching my toddler get so frustrated because the star would not go into the place meant for the triangle, and the round peg wouldn't fit into the square space, no matter how hard he tried. Angry and overwhelmed, he sent the toy flying across the room. Have you ever experienced that degree of frustration in your attempts to master the toy we call life? You tried to push something into the hole in your heart marked "satisfaction" that just didn't fit.

Or if it seemed to fit, it didn't bring the lasting gratification you were looking for. That changes when a person meets Christ. They discover the longing in their soul is fulfilled in a way they have never experienced before. The freedom and contentment they have in Christ is overwhelming, and for the first time in their lives, they really feel *alive*! The psalmist was right when he proclaimed that the Lord is the One who satisfies the longing soul.

But as true as that is, here is what I find to be interesting. As I look around, surveying the landscape of the body of Christ, from pastors to parishioners, I still see many discontent Christians. You hear it in their conversations—the complaining, the critical spirits, the frustration that comes out at any given time. Therefore, one of the great paradoxes in the Christian life is how Jesus can fill the heart with peace and purpose, and yet we can still struggle with feelings of discontentment and discouragement. We continue to long for something more, something better, and something else. I feel it myself, all the time.

Have you ever gone to bed at the end of what seemed like the perfect day, where everything came together and you felt the Lord's pleasure on your life at every turn? You laid your head on the pillow that night, full and satisfied, thankful to be alive and so appreciative to be a child of God. I have had days like that. But then, after a perfect day and a great night's sleep, have you ever woken up the next morning to incredibly strong feelings of wrestling in your soul? The wonder of the previous day seems like a distant memory, and your heart feels anxious and agitated for no apparent reason. You suddenly feel a sense of longing in your heart for something that is so strong, it has your stomach twisted into knots and you can't explain it. *What is going on? Why do I feel this way? Why am I experiencing these longings all over again? Am I really saved? Is there something wrong with me?*

## THREE BUILT-IN LONGINGS

Listen friend, those feelings are normal. In fact, I believe Scripture supports that what you are experiencing is deeply spiritual. You see, as believers, we have a built-in longing for three distinct things that are the result of God's Spirit living within us. The Bible teaches that when we give our lives to Christ, the Holy Spirit of God comes to reside in our hearts (Ephesians 3:17). His presence brings our spirits to life, though they were originally dead because of sin. The Holy Spirit begins a work of transformation because His ultimate goal, according to Romans 8:29, is to change us into the image of Christ. Or to put it another way, His goal is not to make us a better version of ourselves, but to make us more like Jesus. It is the Holy Spirit's presence in our lives that has created the restlessness inside. It is the reason that we can find ourselves at times, though fully saved and blessed, still battling feelings of discontentment and dissatisfaction.

These three distinct longings are:

- intimacy with God
- heaven or eternity
- eternal purpose and impact

Every single day, the Holy Spirit is moving us and stirring our hearts toward those three things. If we understand what we are ultimately longing for, it will help us to better navigate the feelings of discontentment and dissatisfaction we battle against on a regular basis in our everyday lives and circumstances.

For example, we wrestle because there are areas of our marriage that need improving, or our house feels too small for our growing family, or suddenly too big because we are now "empty nesters." Your friend gets a new car, and immediately you feel like your car, which happens to run perfectly, is lacking in some way. You come back from a nice family vacation, only to see a commercial advertising some exotic place, and something in your heart says, *I would have had a nicer time had we gone there.*

Now there is nothing wrong or sinful about wanting to go on a nice vacation or desiring a dependable car, or a more comfortable house to fit the needs of our families. And certainly there is nothing wrong with yearning to see our marriages grow and improve. But these longings can become distracting and damaging, especially if they become our focus and pursuit for satisfaction. Longings can become idols if we somehow think that they are what will really make us happy.

Here is what we must understand: What we are really wanting is not a better marriage or a bigger house or a nicer car or the perfect vacation. At the root, we are longing for a deeper intimacy with Jesus, for our home in heaven, and to have an eternal impact in this world. It is the Holy Spirit Himself who is pushing us toward these three pursuits. Once we grasp hold of this reality and discover how to respond accordingly, our lives are radically changed. In fact, I will be so bold as to say that our lives will never the same!

That is what I plan on unpacking for you in the following chapters of this book. We will look at how and why the Holy Spirit is constantly pushing us toward intimacy with God the Father. We will also bring to light the biblical truth that heaven is not the end-all for the follower of Jesus Christ, and why we need to learn to live with eternity in view. Finally, we will consider how and why the Holy Spirit is always reminding us that we have been redeemed by Jesus to be a visible expression of His invisible grace while living in this fallen world.

As you read the pages of this book, allow the Lord to encourage and challenge your heart, and I believe life, for you, will take on a whole new meaning.

# WHY AM I STILL THIRSTY?

*"And because you are sons, God has sent forth the Spirit of His Son into your hearts, crying out, 'Abba, Father!'"*

GALATIANS 4:6

In 1965, Ray Graves, head football coach from the University of Florida, sat down with a team of university physicians and researchers and asked them to determine why so many of his Florida Gator players were being affected by heat stroke and other heat-related illnesses. The researchers went to work investigating and soon discovered two key factors that were causing the Gator players to wilt.

1.  The fluids and electrolytes that the players lost through sweat were not being replaced.

2.  The large amounts of carbohydrates the players' bodies used for energy were not being replenished.

The researchers then took their findings into the lab and scientifically formulated a new, precisely balanced carbohydrate-electrolyte beverage that would adequately replace the key components lost through sweating and exercise. They called their concoction Gatorade™. The Florida Gators football team credited Gatorade™ as having contributed to their first Orange Bowl win over the Georgia Tech Yellow Jackets in 1967, at which point the drink gained traction within the athletic community. Yellow Jackets Coach, Bobby Dodd, when asked why his team lost, replied: "We didn't have Gatorade™. That made the difference."[1]

Gatorade™ is commonly called the "thirst quencher," but personally, although I like the fact that it helps replenish fluids and electrolytes, I have never been a huge fan. The reason? It makes me thirstier! It is called the thirst quencher, but every time I drink one, I find myself desperately craving water.

## JESUS: THE THIRST QUENCHER?

In my relationship with Jesus, I had a similar experience that really confused me at first. I read in my Bible where Jesus declared, *"I am the bread of life. He who comes to Me shall never hunger, and he who believes in Me shall never thirst"* (John 6:35). I came to Jesus and gave Him my heart. I partook of His bread and His life and experienced a filling and a satisfaction like I had never encountered before. My spiritual thirst was quenched, and I was happy.

But then I experienced something I was not expecting. Several weeks later, I felt incredibly hungry and thirsty again, spiritually speaking, and I wondered what was wrong. Why did I suddenly have this longing in my soul and feel restless? Did something happen? Did I sin in some way? Did Jesus abandon me? Jesus said that if I came to Him, I would never hunger or thirst again, so why did I feel this lack of fulfillment? Those questions plagued me, and I know they trouble many other believers as well. So what is the problem?

I have since discovered that Jesus' statement in John 6:35 meant something completely different than I initially thought. I was thinking that if I partake of Jesus, I will never have to eat again. I will never thirst again. But He was in essence saying, *Come to Me, and*

23

*you will have an endless supply of nourishment to satisfy your hungry soul. Believe in Me and trust in Me and you will experience a reservoir of life to quench your thirsty heart.* The idea is that we are to simply keep coming to Him. The more we come, the more He fills and satisfies us. And the more we come, the hungrier we get!

You see, eating and drinking spiritually is the opposite of eating and drinking physically. Physically speaking, when you eat, you get full. How many of us have declared after a delicious Thanksgiving meal, where we have definitely committed the sin of gluttony, that we are never going to eat again? But that only lasts for a couple of hours until someone announces that it's time for dessert. Then suddenly, without even thinking, we are stuffing ourselves until we are completely full and feeling sick. Eating food makes you full, but the opposite is true, spiritually speaking. When you partake of Jesus, the more you eat, the hungrier you become. That is the beauty of John 6:35. Jesus is not saying that you will never be spiritually hungry again when you come to Him, but rather that in Him, you will have an endless supply of the nourishment that you crave. Jesus is announcing that the supply never runs dry! He is always ready to fill and satisfy the longing heart. His Holy Spirit within us is constantly stirring up that hunger for more of Jesus and a deeper intimacy in our relationship with Him.

## THE SIGNIFICANCE OF ABBA

The apostle Paul gives us some profound insight into this reality. When writing to the believers in Galatia, he shares about how they had been set free from slavery to sin and adopted into the family of God. He tells them that God actually refers to believers as His sons and daughters. Then Paul says, *"And because you are sons, God has sent forth the Spirit of His Son into your hearts, crying out, 'Abba, Father'"* (Galatians 4:6).

The reason this statement is so significant is because the term Abba means "Daddy." It is an expression that speaks of an intimate relationship between a father and his child. A Jewish child who lived in the first century would only use this term in the privacy of the family's home. When he was out in public, the child was trained to address his father in a more formal manner like "Sir" or even "Father." But when the child was at home, he was free to say "Abba" or "Daddy." Now don't miss the significance of this. Paul declares that the Holy Spirit is in your heart and *He* is constantly crying out, "Daddy!" Or to put it another way, the Holy Spirit is crying out in a way to draw you into a direction that speaks of a greater intimacy with your heavenly Father, with your Abba.

That is the reason why, when you wake up in the morning, you feel this urge to pick up your Bible and read it and spend some time talking to God. It is not simply because you have heard your pastor talk about the importance of having a daily devotional life or you read in some book how having a quiet time is the best way to start your day. I believe it is so much deeper than that! You wake up and the Holy Spirit is there in your heart crying, "Daddy, can I spend time with You? Daddy, do You have time for me?" Developing intimacy with God is the heartbeat of the Christian life.

## THE MEANING OF ETERNAL LIFE

Jesus prayed, *"And this is eternal life, that they may know You, the only true God, and Jesus Christ whom You have sent"* (John 17:3). When we think of eternal life, we usually think in terms of longevity, that eternal life means that we are going to live forever. But to the Jewish listener, eternal life had a broader and deeper meaning. It not only referred to longevity of life, but it also spoke of a quality of life that begins the moment a person starts following God. Jesus is saying that the quality of life everyone is looking for and desiring is found in knowing God. The New Testament was written in Greek, and the Greek word for *know* is the word *ginōskō*, which basically means to know someone in the deepest and most intimate way. So Jesus is revealing to us that real life, quality life, satisfying and fulfilling life, is found in knowing Him in an intimate way.

The apostle Paul understood this. Before coming to Christ, Paul was known as Saul, a religious Pharisee who hated Jesus and persecuted the church. He was the man who set out on a personal mission to put an end to a sect called "The Way," the term given to the followers of Jesus at that time. In Acts chapter 9, we read that he was armed with authority from the high priest to imprison followers of Christ, and he was on his way to the city of Damascus to fulfill his mission. But on the road, his life was forever changed. A light that was brighter than the sun blinded Saul, and he fell to the ground and heard a voice asking, *"Saul, Saul, why are you persecuting Me?"* Saul answered, *"Who are You, Lord?"* and *"What do You want me to do?"* (Acts 9:4–6). Those two questions would become Paul's passion and pursuit for the rest of his life. From that point on, Paul was pursuing Jesus with every ounce of his being. He lived to know Jesus and to make Him known to the world. Ironically, Paul's relentless pursuit of follower's of Christ before his conversion turned into a relentless pursuit of Jesus after his conversion.

At the end of his life, and after serving Jesus for thirty years, Paul wrote to the church in Philippi, *"Brethren, I do not count myself to have apprehended; but one thing I do, forgetting those things which are behind and reaching forward to those things which are ahead, I press toward the goal for the prize of the upward call of God in Christ Jesus"* (Philippians 3:13–14).

The first time I read those words, I thought to myself, *Paul, you've walked with Jesus for thirty years. Don't you know Him by now?* I think if Paul could have answered my question, he would have declared, *Yes, Rob. I know Him. But there is still so much of Jesus to know.* When you read Paul's epistles, describing his passion to know Christ, you discover phrases like "the surpassing greatness" or "the unsearchable riches" or "the multifaceted colors of the grace of God." To Paul, the knowledge of Christ was a treasure chest that had no bottom. Every day was the opportunity to discover another jewel of truth or to see another color in the beauty of Jesus and His incredible plan of redemption. That is the reason Paul's whole life was marked by a passionate pursuit to press into Christ and know Him as deeply as he possibly could.

## PELICANS AND FISH

Years ago, the Lord gave me a vivid picture of Paul's passionate pursuit of Jesus. One morning, I ventured down to the beach for a walk with Jesus and to spend time in His Word. As I sat there reading my Bible, I saw something that I had never seen before in all my years of living by the ocean. A flock of pelicans was flying about fifty yards off the shore, circling in their flight until suddenly, one by one, they dive-bombed straight into the ocean. At first, I had no idea why these giant birds with their huge beaks were throwing themselves, seemingly careless of the consequences, into the ocean. Then, when I saw one of them come up with a large fish in its mouth, I realized what was happening. The pelicans had found a school of fish, and they were having a feeding frenzy! They were throwing themselves into the water with reckless abandon because they had their eyes on a prize, and nothing was going to distract them from reaching their goal.

As I sat there, mesmerized for about forty-five minutes while watching this ordeal, the Lord quietly, but strongly, spoke to my heart. "Rob, I want you to pursue Me with that same kind of reckless abandon. Eye on the prize. All in. Holding nothing back!"

In 1 Corinthians 9:24–27, Paul compares the Christian life to running a race and to boxing. He says that when he is running, he has his eye on the prize. And when he is boxing, he is not just punching the air, but he is seeking to hit a target. It is a great analogy because the Christian life is meant to be lived with purpose. We are to be aiming for a prize. We are not running just to run. We are running to win! What is the prize? It is Jesus Himself and all that is found in knowing Him.

That day on the beach was a turning point in my pursuit of Christ. However, I will readily admit that I do not always pursue knowing Jesus with that "all in" reckless abandon. There are plenty of days where I find myself running just to run, not having my eye on the prize. Many times, the things of this world, and the consumerism that is such a big part of it, distract me. Sometimes I find myself falling into the trap of thinking, *What I really need is to enjoy some entertainment. I need a change of scenery. A nice vacation in Maui is what I am really craving.* Now again, please do not misunderstand me. I don't think there is anything wrong with entertainment. I enjoy a good movie or sporting event, and they definitely help get my mind off of the pressures in my life for an hour or two. One of my favorite things to do in life is to vacation in Maui with my wife, resting and snorkeling, enjoying an amazing place that God created. But what we desperately need to understand is that entertainment, vacations, and anything else associated with life in this world is not what we are really longing for. Nothing in this life will bring lasting satisfaction.

The only One who can truly satisfy the longing in our souls is Jesus, and that is why every single day when we wake up, the Holy Spirit is there in our hearts crying out, "Daddy," seeking to remind us that Jesus loves us and is waiting for us, and that Jesus is interested in our hearts. He is longing for us to grow in our relationship with Him! What makes a great vacation is the time spent away from the distractions of everyday life, getting to spend extra time with the Lord. The Bible declares, *"He is a rewarder of those who diligently seek Him"* (Hebrews 11:6). The number one thing that He rewards us with is more of Himself. Jeremiah 29:13 puts it this way, *"You will seek Me and find Me, when you search for Me with all of your heart."*

The sad reality for too many Christians is that they merely scratch the surface of what it really means to know Christ and live in relationship with Him. They don't view the knowledge of Christ, and knowing Him like Paul did, as this bottomless treasure chest of riches—one that they can spend their entire life looking into, and thus experience the wealth and beauty of life in Christ. If you think that is a harsh or unfair statement, consider these two prayers of Paul concerning believers in the church in Ephesus. Ask yourself how many of the words in bold are a reality in your Christian experience.

> *Therefore I also, after I heard of your faith in the Lord Jesus and your love for all the saints, do not cease to give thanks for you, making mention of you in my prayers: that the God of our Lord Jesus Christ, the Father of glory, may give to you the spirit of wisdom and revelation in the knowledge of Him, the* **eyes of your understanding being enlightened; that you may know what is the hope of His calling,** *what are the* **riches of the glory of His inheritance in the saints,** *and what is the* **exceeding greatness of His power toward us who believe,** *according to the working of His*

*mighty power which He worked in Christ when He raised Him from the dead and seated Him at His right hand in the heavenly places, far above all principality and power and might and dominion, and every name that is named, not only in this age but also in that which is to come. And He put all things under His feet, and gave Him to be head over all things to the church, which is His body, the fullness of Him who fills all in all.*

—Ephesians 1:15–23

A famous writer named Alexander Pope wrote, "Know then thyself, presume not God to scan; the proper study of mankind is man."[2] Charles Spurgeon responded to this famous statement: "It has been said by someone that 'the proper study of mankind is man.' I will not oppose the idea, but I believe it is equally true that the proper study of God's elect is God; the proper study of a Christian is the Godhead. The highest science, the loftiest speculation, the mightiest philosophy which can ever engage the attention of a child of God, is the name, the nature, the person, the work, the doings, and the existence of the great God whom he calls his Father."[3]

What do you really know of the hope of His calling? What do you really know of the riches of the glory of His inheritance in the saints and the exceeding greatness of His power toward us who believe, a power that Paul declares raised Jesus Christ from the dead?

My point in asking these questions is not to be condemning but to stir up within your heart a great desire to respond to the promptings of the Holy Spirit to get to know Jesus more. I personally can attest that I don't know enough of these blessings that are ours in Christ, and too often what I do know doesn't shape the way I live.

Paul would further pray in Ephesians 3:14–19:

*"For this reason I bow my knees to the Father of our Lord Jesus Christ, from whom the whole family in heaven and earth is named, that He would grant you, according to the riches of His glory, to be strengthened with might through His Spirit in the inner man, that Christ may dwell in your hearts through faith; that you, being rooted and grounded in love, may be able to comprehend with all the saints what is the* **width** *and* **length** *and* **depth** *and* **height***—to know* **the love of Christ which passes knowledge***; that you may be filled with all the fullness of God."*

I love how Paul hits upon every facet of the love of Christ in this description—width, height, length, and depth. Then to really make his point, he adds, "*to know the love of Christ which passes knowledge."* Once again, this is the great apostle who is speaking, arguably the most devout Christian who has ever lived. He was given incredible spiritual insight to pen three-fourths of the New Testament, and in speaking of the love of Christ, he calls it a love that surpasses knowledge. In other words, it is a love that we can spend the rest of our lives exploring and still not hit bottom. I don't know about you, but I find that incredibly exciting!

Being filled with the fullness of God takes place as we respond to the urgings of the Holy Spirit to grow in a more intimate relationship with Christ. In the next chapter, we will discuss the practical ways to make this happen. But for now, I encourage you to put the book down and take a walk with Jesus. Let Him know that you want to be closer to Him. If you have taken your eyes off of the prize of knowing Jesus, confess that to Him, and purpose in your heart to begin to pursue Him with a greater fervency and passion.

# PURSUING
# JESUS

*"But one thing is needed, and Mary has chosen that good part, which will not be taken away from her."*

LUKE 10:42

When the first *Rocky* movie came out in November of 1976, I was in the seventh grade, and I instantly became a lifelong fan of the movie saga. Once, while I was laid up for weeks after having major hip surgery, I watched four *Rocky* movies in one day as inspiration for my long and painful rehabilitation. A new obsession started with that first movie. I distinctly remember one night going to bed, determined that I was going to wake up the next morning before the sun came up to begin my training regimen. When the alarm sounded at 5 a.m., I sprung out of bed, threw on my grey sweatshirt, grey sweat pants, and my black beanie (just like Rocky wore in the movie), and set out on my morning run.

The air was crisp but it felt good. My plan was to run to the park by my house, then take the park trail, making a two-mile loop back to my house. I was off to a great start to what I thought would become a daily habit. Since this was the days before iPods and portable MP3 players, I imagined the *Rocky* soundtrack in my head as I ran. Occasionally, I threw a few boxing jabs as I envisioned Rocky in training. When I reached the park trail, I noticed it wasn't lit up by any streetlights, but that didn't matter because I was running with determination ... until I heard a sound in the darkness that changed everything.

My running had stirred a pack of dogs that were hanging out in the park, and although I couldn't see them, I could hear them barking and running in my direction. Now, I'm not a fan of dogs because I was bit in the face by a German shepherd when I was a kid, so I have always been cautious around them, especially big ones, and these sounded big. So I immediately turned around and hightailed it out of that park as fast as I could before those dogs could eat me for breakfast! I ran straight home, into my bedroom, threw off my shoes and sweats, and jumped back into bed, thus ending my planned training regimen.

Since that day, I have had many starts and stops to my efforts to add regular exercise to my life. Getting in shape physically involves choices and discipline. The same is true when it comes to growing strong in the Lord. A movie or a professional athlete may inspire us to get in shape, but there is something far greater than that seeking to inspire us to draw near to Christ. The Holy Spirit in our hearts is beckoning us, on a regular basis, toward intimacy. However, the only way that intimacy is going to happen will be based upon our choices.

## AN INTIMATE MOMENT IN BETHANY

We see a great example of this principle in the Gospel of Luke. In chapter 10, we find Jesus and His disciples in the town of Bethany, at the home of Mary and Martha and their brother Lazarus. There's a Bible study of sorts going on, and Jesus is sharing truths from the Word with His friends and disciples. The atmosphere is one where all eyes are focused on Jesus, except Martha's. She's in the kitchen preparing a meal for Jesus and His followers. Now, most ladies can relate to this scene—imagine if Jesus and His disciples suddenly showed up at your house! You would probably feel obligated and delighted to serve them. So Martha was busy serving, when somewhere in the midst of all the work, she suddenly wondered, *Why am I doing this all by myself? Where is my sister Mary?*

As she looks around the room, she sees Mary sitting at the feet of Jesus, soaking up every word, and Martha becomes extremely agitated.

The text in Luke's Gospel describes Martha this way: "*[She] was distracted with much serving*" (Luke 10:40a). I find that rather interesting, since Martha was serving Jesus. But I think all of us can find ourselves wrestling with the same issue: distracted in our service *for* Jesus from what is most important *to* Jesus. And what is that? The story in Luke's Gospel answers the question for us.

What happens next is comical and surprising all at the same time. Martha marches right into the room, obviously without even thinking or considering what she was about to do, and interrupts Jesus while He is teaching. She blurts out, "*Lord, do You not care that my sister has left me to serve alone?*" (verse 40b). In her distraction, Martha is not only being critical of Mary but she thinks that Jesus doesn't care about her. And the same thing can happen to us when we get sidetracked by service. We can become critical of others and doubt the Lord's love and care for us.

Imagine the room after Martha's sudden outburst: I picture it being filled with an awkward silence as people stare at Martha, wondering how she could be so rude. Then others might have been thinking that

Martha had a point. Why was Mary with the men rather than in the kitchen with Martha? Everyone looked at Jesus, anticipating His response.

Jesus' answer is insightful and reveals His heart. He looked at Martha and said, "*Martha, Martha, you are worried and troubled about many things. But one thing is needed, and Mary has chosen that good part, which will not being taken away from her*" (verses 41–42). What was Mary doing? She was sitting at the feet of Jesus. In other words, Mary put herself in a place where she could be close to Jesus and hear from Him. His reply tells us that in order to develop intimacy with Jesus, we must choose to sit at His feet and hear His heart. It also reveals to us a very important truth about life in the Lord, especially for those who are engaged in some form of service—ministry can be taken away from us, but nothing can take away the intimacy we develop with the Lord when we choose to spend time with Him. Ministries will end and projects will be completed. So, if we are finding our identity in a ministry role rather than in who we are in Christ and who Christ wants to be in us, we are not only missing the point, but we are setting ourselves up for a major fall.

## FIRST LOVE?

Most Christians know that spending time with Jesus and developing a devotional life is important.

However, most would also admit that it is easier said than done. The reason is because our lives are full. The demands of life, the responsibilities of work and raising a family, while trying to stay sane amidst a myriad of activities that compete for our time and attention, make spending time with Jesus a challenge. This, so often, is where the frustration sets in because we sense this longing in our heart to be closer to the Lord. We know what it can be like when we hear Him speak to our hearts.

We go to church and hope to experience Him there, but if we are honest, that can be hit or miss, depending on outside factors. Sometimes our daily reading of the Bible can seem more like a mechanical routine than a passionate pursuit! To make matters worse, something inside of us tells us it should be better than this.

There are even times when we start to wonder if we have become like Ephesus, the church who left their first love. Jesus wrote a letter to this church in Revelation chapter 2. This fellowship of believers was like Martha, busy serving Jesus. There was a lot of good ministry and activities going on. They were passionate about doctrine and making sure that they believed the right things about Jesus. But Jesus had a problem with them. After commending them for everything that they were doing right, He declared, *"Nevertheless, I have this against you, that you have left your first love*" (Revelation 2:4). Notice, Jesus didn't say they lost it. He said they left it. In other words, at some point in the process of following Jesus and serving Jesus, they walked away from the relationship aspect of what they were doing. They lost sight of the fact that it's all about relationship. He saved us, first and foremost, because He loves us and wants to live in relationship with us. Jesus instructed this church on how to get back to their first love. They were to:

- Remember from where they had fallen
- Repent (have a change of attitude, heart, and direction about their condition)
- Return to their first works

*Remember, Repent, and Return* is the remedy for restoring our first love.

## QUALITY VERSUS QUANTITY

Quite a few years back, I remember hearing a pastor teach on this passage. I definitely felt convicted that, at the very least, if I hadn't left my first love, I was not as "in love" with Jesus as I once was. I knew something needed to change. The pastor's advice was to think back to the time in our lives when we were most in love with the Lord, recall what we were doing, and then start doing those same things again. I found that advice to be more frustrating than helpful because when I thought back to the time when I "felt" the most in love with the Lord, it was during my freshman year of college.

I had stopped playing college baseball and had started studying God's Word more because He had called me into ministry. I went from spending twenty to thirty minutes mechanically reading my Bible to spending several hours devouring God's Word. My heart was on fire! I would often head down to the beach after school to read and pray. It was an amazing time of spiritual refreshment and renewal in my heart, where God's Word was becoming alive and the sense of His presence and the sensitivity to the voice of His Spirit speaking to my heart was as loud and clear as it has ever been in my life. But it was also during a time when my life was very simple and my responsibilities and pressures were minimal. I was living at home rent free, going to school, working a part-time job for gas and spending money, and serving in a ministry that I loved. I was not carrying the weight and responsibility for how that ministry performed.

So, twenty years later, when I heard that preacher's advice, I became frustrated because my life at forty was filled with so many more pressures and responsibilities. I had a family to lead and a wife and kids to devote time and attention to. I had a ministry to oversee and employees to guide and be concerned about. There were bills to pay, and quite frankly, I didn't have the time to go and sit at the beach and seek Jesus three to four times a week, let alone spend countless hours each day in Bible study for my own personal edification. I had messages to prepare and people and ministries to pray for. The stark reality was that my life no longer just involved me and Jesus. So how could I return and do those first works again?

As I prayed about this, the Lord began to speak to my heart that the issue was not so much about the quantity of time spent with Him but the quality of time spent with Him. God was fully aware that I could not spend the same amount of time with Him each day at this stage of my life. He knew the responsibilities before me because it was He who had led me into the ministry and had blessed me with my wife and family. The questions I needed to ask myself weren't based upon the quantity of time, but the quality of our time together.

- Was it focused or distracted?
- Was it passionate or mechanical?
- Was it prompting me to interact with Him throughout the day?

I began evaluating my approach toward devotions and the manner in which I set aside time to spend with Jesus. I discovered that my time with Him needed to be, first of all, *consistent*. For me, that meant every morning. David declared, *"Early will I seek you"* (Psalm 63:1). I have found that starting my day early with Jesus is the best. I also discovered that I needed to keep my devotional time fresh, so I learned to be creative and switch it up from time to time in order to keep it from getting stale. Consequently, I have included many different Bible study methods into my rotation every few months.

I see a similarity in my relationship with my wife. Although we have been married since 1986, we still date one other. And in our dating relationship, we have to be intentional about trying new restaurants or picking new things to do on our day off in order to keep things fresh and vibrant. Sometimes we go through seasons where we take turns planning our date, and whoever is planning tries to pick something new that they think is really going to bless the other person. My wife is my best friend, and there is no one in this world that I enjoy being with more, no one else with whom I am more deeply connected. But being intentional not to fall into routines that could cause our relationship to become stale is an ongoing challenge. It was especially difficult in those years when our kids were young and the demands of work and family made quality time hard to come by. Even though we would spend some time together every day and talk regularly, we learned the value of periodically setting aside a weekend or special occasion to get away, not only for quality time together, but some quantity of time where we could rekindle our love, passion, and intimacy with one other.

I have found this to be just as crucial in my relationship with the Lord. Because of the demands of life, it's necessary for me to periodically schedule an entire day where I have one purpose—time alone with Jesus. I usually try to incorporate some sort of exercise, and the day might move from one location to another. I pick places where there is little or no distraction so I can pray, read, write, and sing if I want to, being so thankful that Jesus doesn't care about my lousy voice. I disconnect from technology so that it's just Jesus, my Bible, my journal, and possibly a book aimed at my heart more than my head. I have found that these days stir up the fire of love in my heart for the Lord. And they improve the quality of my normal, daily devotions even when I lack the quantity. I've also discovered that in these times set apart, a deep and rich connection happens with the Lord as I experience that longing of the Holy Spirit moving me toward Abba. Dissatisfaction grows in intensity, to the point where I begin to sense, weeks ahead of time, the Spirit of God prompting my heart for quality and quantity time, and I need to look at the calendar to see how to make that happen.

Our hearts are restless for more of Jesus, and the more we seek Him, the more we begin to understand what we are really living for—that our purpose for life is living in relationship with Him. Augustine, the great theologian, said in his work, *The Confessions (Book I)*: "*You have formed us for Yourself, and our hearts are restless till they find rest in You.*"[4]

## 4

# BATTLING THROUGH
# THE DRY TIMES

*"Oh, that someone would give me a drink of the
water from the well of Bethlehem, which is
by the gate!"*

2 SAMUEL 23:15

It was 110 degrees at the Little League baseball complex in San Bernardino that day, and I was twelve years old. We were playing a baseball game, and to be honest, I don't remember what team we were playing or who won. But I do have four distinct memories. First, it was a tie score that took the game into extra innings. Second, the game went fifteen innings, over twice as long as a normal Little League game. Third, I pitched a few good innings and my lifelong friend, Phil Eastman, played catcher. And lastly, I was thirsty the entire game! It didn't matter what I drank—Gatorade™, water, soda, or even if I chewed packs of gum—nothing seemed to quench my thirst that day. Playing any kind of sport in that type of weather is absolutely brutal. If it were today, where players have died from heat stroke, I am sure that game would never have been played! That baseball game went on and on, inning after inning, but we got up and kept going back onto the field until the game was over.

## A WALK OF FAITH

In the Christian life, the desert and dry times can also be brutal—those seasons when God's presence seems so distant and we feel completely dry and feeble. It's in those times that we can become discouraged and ready to quit. We might even wonder if we are still saved! I have had many dry spells in my Christian life, and I have learned some important lessons about how to deal with them. The first lesson is that we walk by faith and not by sight, feelings, or emotions.

We have faith in Jesus' promise that He will never leave us or forsake us. We have faith that God's Word won't return void; that even when we can't sense what it is doing, we trust His Word is accomplishing something in our hearts every time we open it. Just as my teammates and I had to keep getting up and going out to play the game, regardless of the heat and fatigue, the same principle applies to approaching God's Word in the desert times. We have to persevere and keep getting up and opening God's Word, regardless of the circumstances or how we feel, because like that baseball game, the dry time will come to an end.

## LEARN TO BREAK THROUGH

I remember distinctly the first real dry time I went through spiritually. It happened during that freshman year of college, after six straight months of God's Word being more alive to me than ever before. I was spending hours reading and studying the Scriptures and just couldn't seem to put the Bible down because God was speaking profoundly to my heart on every page.

But I remember getting up one morning and reading Hebrews chapter 13 and getting nothing out of it. I thought that maybe I was distracted, so I read the chapter again, this time out loud to help my mind better engage, but it was the same result—nothing. I closed my Bible and went off into my day thinking, *it must just be a bad day.* The next morning I decided to read that same chapter again and to my surprise, I got nothing—no nugget; no truth; no insight. I didn't feel like God was speaking to my heart at all. So, I closed my Bible and went about my day thinking, *It's just another bad day. Nothing to worry about.*

On day three, I once again opened my Bible to Hebrews chapter 13 and began to read, and to my shock, it was the same result—I GOT NOTHING! I thought that maybe Hebrews 13 was just a "dry" chapter, so I decided to continue on with my reading and started the book of James, which is always good and insightful, right? Not this time. Instead, I experienced the same result. I might as well have been reading my Bible in a different language, that's how dry it was. It felt as if the voice of God suddenly went silent. I started to panic, wondering if I had sinned in some way that made the Lord cut off fellowship from me. My go-to books were 1 and 2 Samuel; I always got something out of the life of David. So I began to read them, but to my shock and chagrin, even the life of David was like a desert.

This went on for about ten days, and I was getting more and more discouraged. That Sunday at church, I heard a message about the time in Jacob's life when he wrestled with the Lord (although Jacob didn't know who he was wrestling with at that point). The wrestling match went on all through the night, and as morning was dawning, Jacob grabbed a hold of his foe and declared, "I am not letting go until you bless me!" Now, although this was not the main point of the story, his plea jumped out at me. I realized that that was exactly the attitude I needed to have as it related to the dry season in my devotional life.

I went home that day, walked straight into my room, and sat in my chair. I opened my Bible to Hebrews 13 and said to the Lord, "I am not getting out of this chair or leaving this room until You bless me. I need You to speak to my heart through Your Word." I sat there and read the same chapter over and over again, wrestling with my flesh, my attention span, and my frustration. In tears, I pleaded with Him to speak to me; and for forty-five straight minutes, I heard nothing. But then it happened.

In an instant, it was as if someone broke open the dam and the water of God's Word started rushing over my heart. I picked up my journal and began to write, but I couldn't write fast enough. God was speaking to me through every single verse, and I felt like the Shekinah glory of God invaded my bedroom that day. I was crying and laughing and rejoicing all at the same time. And in that moment, the Lord gently spoke to my heart and said, "Rob, it is not always going to be easy. There will be times when you will have to battle to break through."

This lesson is one that every believer must learn. There are going to be times when you will have to work to build your spiritual muscles and battle to break through. It wasn't that God was playing hard to get or that He was seeking to punish me. It was actually the opposite. He was seeking to transform me and teach me how to persevere spiritually. God was reminding me that "*He is a rewarder of those who diligently seek Him*" (Hebrews 11:6). On this occasion, the emphasis was learning the meaning of diligence.

## DRY TIMES ENHANCE OUR THIRST FOR GOD

I also came to understand that another reason God kept silent was so that I would become thirstier. With each passing day that went by in silence, I was not only getting more frustrated, my thirst for Jesus was increasing. Just like on that hot day at the Little League game, where it seemed that nothing I drank could quench my thirst, it became more apparent during that dry time that Jesus was the only One who could quench my spiritual thirst.

I have experienced many more dry seasons in my devotional life and walk with Jesus since that day, but I have learned not to panic. I realize dry times are part of the process to increase my spiritual thirst and appetite. I have also discovered that if the dry time doesn't subside after a few days, I need to set aside a specific day where I can go somewhere alone to "wrestle" with the Lord" and say to Him again, "I am not leaving this place until You bless me." The Lord is drawn to the heart that is desperate for Him, and the Holy Spirit in our hearts who cries out, "Abba Father," is always seeking to keep us in that childlike state where we rely upon the Lord completely for our life, sustenance, and being.

Over and over again, the Bible encourages us to live our lives fully dependent upon God. But that can be hard for us, especially for men, because from the time that we were little tikes, we were constantly being told to grow up and be independent from our parents. The natural tendency in all of us is to "make it on our own" and be independent, but the Bible teaches us a completely different principle. The Bible says that, "*In Him we live and move and have our being*" (Acts 17:28). Jesus put it this way to His disciples in John 15, "*I am the vine, you are the branches. He who abides in Me, and I in him, bears much fruit; for without Me you can do nothing*" (verse 5). Dry seasons are God's way of reminding us of our need to stay connected to the vine and to be gaining our nourishment from Jesus alone. Seeking His heart becomes the way our lives bring glory to Him.

## A BREAKTHROUGH STORY

In 2 Samuel 23 we see a great story of breakthrough involving David and a few of his men. The scene takes place during the time when David was on the run from King Saul and hiding out in the caves of Adullam. The Philistines had taken possession of the city of

Bethlehem, and as David was hiding out in the cave, someone overheard him say, "*What I wouldn't give for a drink of water from the well in Bethlehem!*" (see verse 15). No sooner had David said those words when three of his mighty men left the cave and set out on foot to sneak into the city of Bethlehem to get water out of that well for their beloved friend and king. The passage tells us that these three men risked life and limb, somehow breaking through the garrison of the Philistines, to get David a drink. They were so in tune with the heart of David, they made it their priority and passion to fulfill his wish.

The interesting thing about this story is that the passage doesn't tell us how they broke through, only that they *did* break through. I think there is a reason why the Lord doesn't tell us. He knows that we are so prone to develop formulas and methods for our Christian experience that, if we knew exactly how these guys broke through, we would create a formula to follow. But in reality, He wants us all to learn how we need break through and to realize it might be different each time. The most important thing is for us to understand the significance of living life to please Jesus, our King, just like these men wanted to please David. We also must realize our need to learn how to break through in our devotional life, in responding to the Holy Spirit's built-in longing in our hearts for intimacy with God. The more we respond to the cries of Abba in our heart, the thirstier we will become for His presence, His will, and His way to permeate every single area of our lives.

Acknowledging that the first thing we are longing for is intimacy with God plays into the second built-in longing, which is for heaven itself. We are told in 1 Corinthians 13:12 that right now, we see through a glass dimly. But there is a day and time coming where we will see clearly. Right now, we know in part. But when we arrive in heaven, we are going to know all things.

In the next chapter, we will begin to explore how the Holy Spirit is constantly seeking to move us in a direction and mindset of living with eternity in view!

5

# A LONGING
# FOR HEAVEN

*"Now He who has prepared us for this very thing*
*is God, who also has given us the Spirit*
*as a guarantee."*

2 CORINTHIANS 5:5

I have been blessed throughout my life to travel to many great places on this planet that display God's creative handiwork. Missionary trips have taken me from the green, rolling hills of England and New Zealand to the sandy beaches of Costa Rica and Australia. I have seen the beauty of Victoria Falls in Zimbabwe as well as the magnificent mountains of Austria. My wife and I have vacationed on the beaches of Maui and Cabo, Mexico, and also in the lush, green mountains of Oregon. My travels constantly remind me that even though the earth has been impacted by sin, to the point that it is but a fraction of its original beauty, it is still a stunning place! Yet every time I experience a new wonder, a sense still fills my heart that I am destined to a greater place and calling than anything this world has to offer. The Spirit of God in our hearts refuses to allow us to get too comfortable on this planet because, quite frankly, this world is not our home.

## A LONGING BRIDE

In 2 Corinthians chapter 5, Paul the apostle gives an interesting picture of the longing that is in our hearts for heaven and what awaits believers on the other side.

> For we know that if our earthly house, this tent, is destroyed, we have a building from God, a house not made with hands, eternal in the heavens. For in this we groan, earnestly desiring to be clothed with our habitation which is from heaven, if indeed, having been clothed, we shall not be found naked. For we who are in this tent groan, being burdened, not because we want to be unclothed, but further clothed, that mortality may be swallowed up by life. Now He who has prepared us for this very thing is God, who also has given us the Spirit as a guarantee. So we are always confident, knowing that while we are at home in the body we are absent from the Lord.

*For we walk by faith, not by sight. We are confi-
dent, yes, well pleased rather to be absent from
the body and to be present with the Lord.*

—2 Corinthians 5:1–8

What a glorious promise the Lord makes for us!
In eternity, we receive a new body that is not affected
by the elements of this life, namely: time, disease, and
death. If you are over the age of forty, you can identify with Paul's sentiment about the body groaning because you wake up with a daily reminder of this truth.
When you sit down for breakfast over a bowl of cereal
and hear "snap," "crackle," and "pop," it's not your cereal making that noise, it's your aging body! The good
news is that there is a day coming when we get to trade
in our old model for the new model—one that is perfect and knows no limitations. I had hip surgery when
I was thirty-six years old, and my body has never been
the same since, so I cannot wait!

Did you notice the profound statement Paul
made in verse 5? "*Now He who has prepared us for
this very thing is God, who also has given us the Spirit
as a guarantee.*" In other words, God is going to make
good on His promise. We are familiar with the idea
of that word *guarantee* because we use it in much the
same way, as a pledge that we will keep our promise.
In first-century culture, the word *guarantee* referred

59

to a down payment. If a man wanted to buy a piece of property, he would put down a certain amount of cash to secure the property, and it was a guarantee that he was coming back with the rest of the money to purchase the field. God has placed His Spirit in our hearts as a down payment, assuring us that He will one day bring us into glory where we will receive the blessing of a new body that has been specifically designed to enjoy eternity to the fullest.

In Greek, *guarantee* could also be translated as an engagement ring. This beautiful word picture gives tremendous insight into the built-in longing that we have for heaven. What happens when a young man meets the girl of his dreams and decides she is the woman he wants to spend the rest of his life with? He starts saving his money. He might even begin to sell some stuff: that old bike he doesn't ride anymore or the extra surfboard that he rarely uses. He may take on extra work so he can get enough money to buy an engagement ring for his love. And then, he plans some special occasion to propose to her. (Over the years at my church, I have seen a trend of young men almost outdoing each other in their efforts to have a unique and wonderful proposal.) When that young man gets down on one knee, he is declaring his love to this girl and his intention to make her his bride. And just so she knows that he is serious about his commitment and promise, he presents her with a beautiful engagement ring!

That is the picture Paul is painting in 2 Corinthians 5. Jesus has declared that we are His betrothed, and the day is coming when He will return for His bride-to-be and take us to the marriage feast in heaven. In the analogy that Paul is using, Jesus is the bridegroom and we are the bride-to-be, and He has given us the Holy Spirit as our engagement ring to guarantee that He is going to make good on His promise to wed us one day.

Now, let's consider for a moment this analogy from the girl's viewpoint. That engagement ring becomes symbolic of the longing in her heart and the anticipation for her wedding day to finally arrive. She cannot wait to be married to the man she loves and to become his bride. The church I pastor is located near the Camp Pendleton Marine Base, where it is not uncommon to see a young, engaged couple separated by distance because of deployment. Oftentimes we see a young woman patiently waiting for her man to come back so that they can be wed, and that engagement ring becomes a symbol of the longing in her heart for that day to approach. If she is out for a walk in the park and passes another couple holding hands and glances down to see their wedding rings, she then looks at her own ring and tells herself, *That is going to be me one day soon. My beloved is coming home, and we are going to be married!*

For those of us who are followers of Christ, we are the bride-to-be in that picture. The engagement ring is symbolic of the Holy Spirit who is constantly longing, not just to escape this fallen world, but more importantly to be united with our Bridegroom, Jesus Christ. His Spirit is relentlessly reminding us that this world is not our home and that there is more to life than meets the eye.

The restlessness we feel at times, even when in the most ideal situations, is because we have been redeemed and rescued by Jesus to dwell with Him in a place that makes the best parts of this world seem like a trash dump in comparison. In 2 Corinthians 12, Paul reflects back on the time when he was taken to heaven in a vision, or some sort of dream (he is not sure). He essentially said that no words in the human vocabulary could even come close to adequately describe what he saw because it was so incredible! The Holy Spirit is well acquainted with heaven and doesn't want to see us settle for second best. The apostle Peter, in his epistle, refers to followers of Jesus as *sojourners* and *pilgrims* in this life (1 Peter 2:11).

Pastor Warren Wierbse, in his book titled *Too Soon to Quit*, gives this great insight: "A vagabond is someone who has no home, a fugitive is someone who is running from home, a stranger is someone who is away from home, and a pilgrim is someone who is headed home."[5] Precious saints, we are pilgrims and sojourners. Our home is in eternity, and this life, with all its good times and bad, is like a short walk in the park compared to what eternity is going to be like.

There was a certain church in the South that was known for its potlucks. They would gather monthly for these love feasts, which included quite a spread of delicious food. It was a great time of eating, laughing, and enjoying fellowship together. As the people went through the buffet line, they were always reminded to save their forks because the best was yet to come, for you see, the desserts were off the charts. One day, a dear sister in the church was stricken with terminal cancer. As her days were drawing to an end, her pastor came for a visit. The woman told him that at her memorial service, she wanted to be laid in her coffin with a fork in her hand, and she wanted them to pass out forks to everyone in attendance. She asked that he would tell the people to keep their heads looking up and focused on Jesus because, "The best was yet to come!"[6]

The Holy Spirit residing in us wants to remind us of this very truth. We have heaven to look forward to and a glorious eternity with our Lord. Remember, believers, heaven is not the "end all." The best is yet to come!

# HEAVEN IS NOT THE END OF THE STORY

*"Blessed and holy is he who has part in the first res-*
*urrection. Over such the second death has no pow-*
*er, but they shall be priests of God and of Christ,*
*and shall reign with Him a thousand years."*

REVELATION 20:6

One of the greatest public servants in the history of England was a man by the name of William Gladstone. Gladstone served as prime minister four times during the latter half of the nineteenth century. He was a committed Christian who always attended church. He also taught a Sunday school class throughout his adult life. In fact, his aim early on was to become an Anglican clergyman, but after his graduation from Oxford, his strong-willed father insisted that he enter politics.

Shortly before he died, Gladstone gave a speech in which he told about being visited by an ambitious young man who sought his advice about life. The lad told the elder statesman that he admired him more than anyone living and wanted career guidance.

"What do you hope to do when you graduate from college?" Gladstone asked.

The young man replied, "I hope to attend law school, sir, just as you did."

"That's a noble goal," said Gladstone. "Then what?"

"I hope to practice law and make a good name for myself defending the poor and the outcasts of society, just as you did."

"That's a noble purpose," replied Gladstone. "Then what?"

"Well, sir, I hope one day to stand for Parliament and become a servant of the people, even as you did."

"That too is a noble hope. What then?" asked Gladstone.

"I would hope to be able to serve in the Parliament with great distinction, evidencing integrity and a concern for justice—even as you did."

"What then?" asked Gladstone.

"I would hope to serve the government as Prime Minister with the same vigor, dedication, vision, and integrity as you did."

"And what then?" asked Gladstone.

"I would hope to retire with honors and write my memoirs—even as you are presently doing—so that others could learn from my mistakes and triumphs."

"All of that is very noble," said Gladstone. "And then what?"

The young man thought for a moment. "Well, sir, I suppose I will then die."

"That's correct," said Gladstone. "And then what?"

The young man looked puzzled. "Well, sir," he answered hesitantly, "I've never given that any thought."

"Young man," Gladstone responded, "the only advice I have for you is for you to go home, read your Bible, and *think about eternity*."[7]

## HEAVEN IS NOT THE END-ALL

To think about eternity is great advice and one of the things I believe the Holy Spirit is urging us to do on a regular basis. One of the biggest misnomers in the church today is the idea that heaven is the end of the story and the final destination for those who put their faith in Christ. But in reality, according to Scripture, heaven is merely a stopover in the greater picture of God's eternal plan for believers.

Now, don't get me wrong. I am totally looking forward to heaven! Jesus spoke of heaven in John chapter 14 as the place that He was going away to and was preparing for us. I can't wait to see heaven with its gold asphalt and the throne of God in all its splendor and glory, as described in the book of Revelation. I am so glad that we have the hope of heaven and verses like Paul's, where the great apostle said, "*We are confident, yes, well pleased rather to be absent from the body and to be present with the Lord*" (2 Corinthians 5:8). I am also thankful that heaven is one of the rewards of the faithful followers of Christ, and I know it is going to be a million times better than I can even imagine. But I am also extremely excited about what follows heaven. "There is something that follows heaven?" you ask. Yes indeed!

The Bible tells us that when Christ comes for His church, in an event known as the rapture, He is going to take us to heaven where we are going to be with Him, celebrating our wedding feast. Now, depending on your view of eschatology and the rapture, your time in heaven varies. I happen to believe in a pre-tribulational view, meaning the rapture will happen prior to the tribulation and that we will be with Jesus in heaven during the seven years of tribulation on planet earth. If you believe in a mid-tribulational view, which states that Jesus comes to rapture the church during the middle of the tribulation (or the three-and-a-half-year mark), then that means you get to spend three-and-a-half years in heaven. If you believe the rapture happens at the end of the tribulation, commonly called the post-tribulational view (or what I like to call the bungee cord view of eschatology), I have bad news for you. You never make it to heaven and you don't get a wedding feast. However, the good news is, no matter what your view of eschatology is, the outcome is the same.

When Jesus returns in power and great glory to the earth at His Second Coming, the Bible makes it clear that His church (bride) is coming with Him. Jesus is going to set up His kingdom here on earth, and we are going to rule and reign with Him for one thousand years. I believe in a literal millennium—one thousand years. This is what we have to look forward to! If you have viewed eternity as an endless feast and worship service, or Hollywood's picture of saints sitting on clouds and playing harps, I have news for you—it is going to be far better than all of that! We are going to enjoy the beauty and wonder of a renewed earth, and we are going to serve alongside Jesus in His millennial reign with position and responsibility. Many places in the Bible speak of this special role that we are going to enjoy. For instance:

*"Who then is a faithful and wise servant, whom his master made ruler over his household, to give them food in due season? Blessed is that servant whom his master, when he comes, will find so doing. Assuredly, I say to you that he will make him ruler over all his goods"* (Matthew 24:45–47).

*"If we endure, we shall also reign with Him"* (2 Timothy 2:12).

*"And he who overcomes, and keeps My works until the end, to him I will give power over the nations—'He shall rule them with a rod of iron; they shall be dashed to pieces like the potter's vessels'— as I also have received from My Father"* (Revelation 2:26–27).

*"Do you not know that the saints will judge the world? And if the world will be judged by you, are you unworthy to judge the smallest matters? Do you not know that we shall judge angels? How much*

*more, things that pertain to this life?"*
*(1 Corinthians 6:2–3).*

This, my believing friend, is our destiny, and we need to realize that the Holy Spirit is seeking to remind us of this truth: the way we live in the here and now is going to play a part in what we do and how we enjoy life in the there and then. Don't get me wrong. I believe all of us are going to enjoy eternity to the fullest. But our capacity of fullness to enjoy it is going to differ. For some, their capacity might be like the size of a Dixie Cup, while for others, it's like a cargo container on a shipping freight—capable of holding tons.

Think of it this way: When my little daughter Amanda was two years old, she liked to pull my wife's pots and pans out of the cupboard and bang them on the floor. She would sit there with a big smile on her face, making what she obviously thought was beautiful noise. That was Amanda at age two, but now Amanda is an adult. She would never get pleasure out of banging pots and pans together, except maybe on New Year's Eve. My point is this: her capacity of enjoyment has changed with maturity. Well, in heaven, everyone is going to be full, but our capacity is going to differ greatly, and it will primarily be determined by what we did in this life, living our lives for Christ and serving Him.

## THE PROLOGUE VERSUS
## THE REAL STORY

A lot of books have what is commonly called the prologue—the story before the real story. The prologue is the setup: it introduces us to the characters and gives us some insight into what the story is going to be about. Well, my friends, this life here on earth is the prologue, but eternity is the real deal. We may live seventy, eighty, or maybe ninety years here, if we are unlucky (sort of kidding; the idea of living past ninety doesn't appeal to me, considering what is waiting around the corner in eternity). But however long we live, it's a blink, a blip on the radar, a breath in comparison to the billion gazillion years in eternity. The concept of eternity is hard for us to comprehend because the Bible is pretty vague about it. But eternity is the real story.

## WE ARE TO BUILD WITH
## ETERNITY IN VIEW

In 1 Corinthians chapter 3, Paul compares the Christian life and Christian service to that of a builder. In verses 10–11, he states that Jesus is the only foundation we can build upon, but we need to take heed as to how we build. The materials we build with play a part in how our labor is measured out in eternity. Paul makes this very clear beginning in verse 12 (NLT):

> *"Anyone who builds on that foundation may use a variety of materials—gold, silver, jewels, wood, hay, or straw. But on the judgment day, fire will reveal what kind of work each builder has done. The fire will show if a person's work has any value. If the work survives, that builder will receive a reward. But if the work is burned up, the builder will suffer great loss. The builder will be saved, but like someone barely escaping through a wall of flames."*

—1 Corinthians 3:12–14

So we can build with a variety of materials, but those materials are going to be tested by fire. What happens to wood, hay, and straw when they are exposed to fire? They burn up; they can't stand the test and are destroyed. But what happens to gold, silver, and jewels when they are exposed to fire? They are able to endure the heat and are actually purified by the fire. What Paul is telling us is that our works, service, attitudes, and actions will one day be tried. Some of them are going to be burned up, while others will remain pure and be part of our reward. Our rewards will then have an impact on our responsibilities in our Lord's kingdom.

So what determines if we are building with gold, silver, and jewels versus wood, hay, and straw? I believe the key is found in our motives. If our motives are self-glorification, being seen and praised by men or making a name for ourselves, then our works, service, and actions are going to be like wood, hay, and straw. But if our motives are to glorify God and to point people to Jesus, then they will be like gold, silver, and precious jewels. It is true that even when our heart's desire is to glorify and point people to Jesus, we can still wrestle with those fleshly tendencies toward wanting to be seen and respected by men.

So the question is, how will any of our works stand the test? The answer is found in what happens to gold and silver when it is placed in the fire—the impurities rise to the surface where they are scraped away, and only the pure gold and silver remains.

You see, God is able to distinguish and decipher that which is pure in motive from that which is impure. He knows what is done with the right heart and actions in the midst of our normal struggles against the flesh to prop oneself up and say, "Look at me!"

THINK ABOUT ETERNITY

As I close this chapter, I want you to think about the interview between William Gladstone and the young man. Gladstone asked, "What do you hope to do when you graduate from college?" You may have already graduated from college and are in a completely different season of life—maybe you are getting married, receiving a job promotion, changing professions, or perhaps moving on to a new ministry assignment. You may even be entering the time of retirement!

Whatever stage of life you are in, I challenge you to ask yourself these questions: What is my goal? What have I set my heart and mind upon? And when I achieve that, what then? Take some time to pause and consider eternity, because eternity is what matters!

# LESSONS FROM
# ABRAHAM

*"If then you were raised with Christ, seek those things which are above, where Christ is, sitting at the right hand of God. Set your mind on things above, not on things on the earth. For you died, and your life is hidden with Christ in God. When Christ who is our life appears, then you also will appear with Him in glory."*

COLOSSIANS 3:1–4

Did you know that, in reality, there are only two ways to live? The most common way is to live by sight—to base everything on what we can see. The other way, which is far less common, is to live by faith, to base our lives ultimately and primarily on what we cannot see. The challenge with living by faith, especially with eternity in view, is the daily grind of life. Every single day, the responsibilities, problems, obstacles, and cares we face obstruct our vision and focus. We have a difficult time seeing the forest through the trees.

## THE HALL OF FAITH

Bible scholars and teachers refer to Hebrews chapter 11 as the "Hall of Faith." This chapter gives us some brief vignettes from the Old Testament of men and women who lived the life of faith. These people lived their lives on planet earth with eternity in view, looking for the place and the life to come, the life that was promised by God. The remarkable thing about these people is that they lived highly effective lives. One of these men was Abraham:

> *"By faith Abraham obeyed when he was called to go out to the place which he would receive as an inheritance. And he went out, not knowing where he was going. By faith he dwelt in the land of promise as in a foreign country, dwelling in tents with Isaac and Jacob, the heirs with him of the same promise; for he waited for the city which has foundations, whose builder and maker is God."*

—Hebrews 11:8–10

LIVING VERTICALLY

We learn several things from the life of Abraham about living in light of eternity. First, Abraham was willing to step out of his comfort zone.

We are introduced to Abram in Genesis chapter 11. Abram (later to be called Abraham) was minding his own business while living in a place called Ur of the Chaldeans. Ur was a place of luxury; in fact, history indicates that hot tubs were first invented there. So Abram was doing his own thing when Jehovah God appeared to him and called him to make a radical change in his lifestyle. God had a proposal for Abram: "Leave your homeland and set out on a journey. I'll tell you where to go as you travel. In that new land, I am going to make a brand-new nation and people group from your descendants. They will be My special people, and they will have a special purpose in the history of the world."

Now, that all sounded pretty amazing to Abram, so he said *yes* to God. He would leave his homeland and set out on this journey of faith, believing in the promise of God to make a new nation from his loins even though he was seventy-five years old and didn't have any children. He also agreed to this plan without talking to his wife, which was another bold move on his part. I am not sure my wife would have been on board, picking up and starting all over when we were well into our seventies. Consider, too, Abram had no idea where he was going and had just met the God who was proposing this brand-new plan. He moved out of his house and chose to live in tents because he was looking for *"the city which has foundations, whose builder and maker is God."* Abraham made a decision to become a promise believer. Every facet of his life would be marked by his firm belief in this one promise from God.

Dr. Herbert Lockyer, a minister and best-selling author, once did a study on the promises of God to the believer found in the Bible. He counted over seven thousand—promises for provision, for faith, for eternity, for ministry. The apostle Paul proclaimed in 2 Corinthians 1:20, *"For all the promises of God in Him are Yes, and in Him Amen, to the glory of God through us."* In other words, all of God's promises are certain and true for every believer because we are positionally placed in Christ. *"For you died, and your life is hidden with Christ in God"* (Colossians 3:3).

So if Abraham was willing to step out of his comfort zone, believing in this one promise of God whom he had just met, how much more should we be willing to step out of our comfort zones, believing the promises of God, to follow the One who gave up everything in order to give us life?

PURSUING COMFORT

So what does this mean practically? How do we live with this vertical perspective? Some would suggest that you have to sell all of your possessions and take a vow of poverty—give up every "thing" to follow Jesus. God has called some people to do that, but not everyone. Possessions are not wrong as long as your possessions don't possess you. What I am suggesting is that we need to divorce ourselves from the world's mindset, which is that our main pursuit should be comfort. Living with a vertical perspective means that I realize my heavenly Father is going to allow things to come into my life that are going to upset my comfort zone, but He is going to use those things to make me more like Jesus and prepare for me eternity.

If you think about it, we jump into many things in life assuming they are going to make us more comfortable. Take for example, marriage. Listen, I love being married to my wife, but getting married did not make my life more comfortable. In fact, life was easier before I got married because I didn't have to take into consideration another person's feelings on most occasions. I could eat what I wanted, when I wanted, and how I wanted. If I ate dessert before dinner, or even dessert *instead* of dinner (two things that drives my wife crazy), there was no one to challenge my eating habits. I could go where I wanted to go and do whatever I wanted to do. I left dishes in the sink, clothes on the floor for days, and stayed up as late as I wanted watching *Sports Center*.

So marriage did not make my lifestyle easier or more convenient, but it did make it better in so many ways. Now I have a best friend on this journey through life, and God uses her to show me things I never realized about myself, or about Him. She encourages me to be a man of God and a man of faith. Quite often, Denise has been the instrument that God has used to point out an area that He wants me to grow in. Now those revelations come not so much from what my wife says to me, but more from the way I react to things that she does that maybe bug or convict me. I often find myself asking the question, *Why did that bug me so much?* Or praying, *Lord, help me to be more caring and compassionate like Denise.*

My point in this illustration is to challenge you to quit thinking about life and pursuits in the context of being comfortable, and instead, think in terms of *becoming better*. Keep in mind the goal of being conformed into a more Christ-centered person. When we separate ourselves from the pursuit of comfort as a means to fulfillment, our perspective changes, and we take on a different mindset. Suddenly, we are more open to doing things like using vacation time and resources to go on a mission trip to a Third World country, or taking a step of faith to volunteer in an area of ministry that we never would have imagined ourselves being involved in, or downsizing in order to invest more into the work and kingdom of God.

Abraham lived as a pilgrim and a sojourner because he believed in the promise of God and was willing to step out of his comfort zone and walk by faith. Because of his decision, Abraham saw God do some amazing things in his life. We, too, can experience the blessings and promises of God unfold in our lives, but it begins with pursuing Him above our own personal comfort.

## ALTARS AND WELLS

There were two things that marked the life of Abraham during his sojourn here on earth that I want to point out. First, he built altars in order to worship God and acknowledge His leadership in his life. Second, he dug wells to care for his family and flocks.

Abraham was a shepherd, and caring for his sheep was his number one responsibility. It was the way he provided for his family. So, as he went through the desert, Abraham was always looking for a water source to tap into. But what I find interesting is that Abraham always built the altars first. And therein lies the secret between taking care of everything on the horizontal plane of our lives and living with eternity in view—we give ourselves to the worship of God first!

Throughout the book of Genesis, we see that wherever Abraham pitched his tent, he built an altar. It was his way of claiming that territory, not for himself, but for God. And because of this, Abraham was never tied down to a particular place. This commitment to building altars was also his way of keeping God at the center of his plans as he journeyed through life, aligning himself with the God of Promise. Abraham was an altar builder; and altars represent the place where the human and the Divine intersect.

- Altars are a place of worship, where we acknowledge the greatness of God.
- Altars are a place of consecration, where we declare plainly that He is greater.
- Altars are a place of sacrifice, where we lay down our lives and declare that we want His will and His way.

## PUTTING YOUR IDENTITY ON THE ALTAR

After Abraham left Ur of the Chaldeans, he wandered in the wilderness for twenty-plus years, all the while, waiting for God to give him a son to fulfill His promise and start the whole process of this new nation. Imagine going year after year without the birth of a son. Imagine the doubts that must have filled Abraham's heart, and the sleepless nights as he would lie awake next to his wife Sarah, thinking to himself, *what have I done?*

When Abraham would meet a stranger and be asked where he was from and why he left his homeland, Abraham would then tell the story of how God visited him and told him to pack up and journey to a land He would lead him to. And Abraham would share about the promise that God had made to him, to produce from his loins a brand new nation. But imagine the reaction of the stranger when he finds out that Abraham doesn't have a son. In fact, he doesn't have any children! Not only that, but Abraham has been on this journey for twenty years and is now in his eighties, and he is still waiting for this promise to come to pass. I am sure that most everyone who met Abraham and heard his story thought he was mad!

But then, it happened. Isaac, the promised child was born! His birth was quite a miracle because Sarah was way beyond the age of bearing children. Now, any time that Abraham was asked about his story and his journey, he could introduce Isaac to the enquirer as the promised child, the one through whom God was going to fulfill His promise. Isaac became the evidence that the plan was in motion and that Abraham wasn't crazy. He really did hear from God. Finally, he could be called "Father Abraham."

But then a pivotal moment came in Abraham's life, one that solidified his faith and commitment to live vertically. It was the day he put that which represented his identity on the altar. Hebrews 11:17–18 records it this way, "*By faith Abraham, when he was tested, offered up Isaac, and he who had received the promises offered up his only begotten son, of whom it was said, 'In Isaac your seed shall be called.'*"

Once Isaac had grown into a young man, God tested Abraham by asking him to take Isaac, his only son and the representation of his entire identity, and sacrifice him on the altar. If Abraham obeyed God and sacrificed his son, he would go down in history as the guy who not only left everything because he thought he heard from God, but the psycho dad who murdered the very son who was supposed to be the fulfillment of the promise!

Yet, Abraham was willing to sacrifice Isaac because he was confident in the promise of God who called him. Hebrews 11:19 ends with this interesting insight—Abraham was willing to put Isaac on the altar because he believed that if God had him go through with this, then God would raise his son from the dead. Abraham was prepared to put his own identity on the altar because he believed in the identity and the power and the love of God! In other words, Abraham's identity was going to be defined by his faith and relationship in God alone, and nothing else.

I believe that a huge part of living with a vertical perspective in this world is realizing God does not exist for us, but we exist for God. The Bible declares that everything was made by Jesus and for Jesus. "*For by Him all things were created that are in heaven and that are on earth, visible and invisible, whether thrones or dominions or principalities or powers. All things were created through Him and for Him*" (Colossians 1:16). Revelation 4:11 tells us that we were made for His pleasure. The purpose of our lives is to bring glory to God. The Holy Spirit in our hearts is constantly seeking to remind us that this world is not our home, that we are pilgrims and sojourners here, and that we exist for a far greater purpose than to live to gratify ourselves. We exist to be a part of the eternal plan and mission of our heavenly Father. The only way that we can ever truly begin to walk in the purpose of our existence is by finding our identity in who we are in Christ.

In Philippians 3:7–14, Paul describes his outlook and focus on life when he declares:

> "*But what things were gain to me, these I have counted loss for Christ. Yet indeed I also count all things loss for the excellence of the knowledge*

*of Christ Jesus my Lord, for whom I have suf-
fered the loss of all things, and count them as
rubbish, that I may gain Christ and be found in
Him, not having my own righteousness, which is
from the law, but that which is through faith in
Christ, the righteousness which is from God by
faith; that I may know Him and the power of His
resurrection, and the fellowship of His sufferings,
being conformed to His death, if, by any means,
I may attain to the resurrection from the dead.
Not that I have already attained, or am already
perfected; but I press on, that I may lay hold of
that for which Christ Jesus has also laid hold of
me. Brethren, I do not count myself to have apprehended; but one thing I do, forgetting those
things which are behind and reaching forward
to those things which are ahead, I press toward
the goal for the prize of the upward call of God
in Christ Jesus."*

Paul states that his life was all about knowing
Jesus, growing in Jesus, and experiencing Jesus. But
there is one phrase that Paul uses in this passage that
really intrigues me; it is the phrase, "*I press on, that
I may lay hold of that for which Christ Jesus has also
laid hold of me.*"

Some translations use the term *apprehended* me in
place of *laid hold* of me. I like that description. Paul was

indeed apprehended by Jesus on the road to Damascus, but why? I believe the reasons were revealed as an ongoing revelation. Every new city he went to, every personal encounter he had, and every new opportunity to share about Jesus was an answer to the question of why Jesus had laid a hold of Paul, and the same is true for you and me. The reason Jesus apprehended us is an ongoing revelation. Every day we are presented with new possibilities and divine encounters that continue to impart the reason for our apprehension, and that ongoing revelation helps satisfy the built-in longing we have for eternal purpose and impact.

We will discuss this more in the following chapter, but as I close this one, please consider these spiritual realities: this world is not your home; you are only visiting this planet. You exist for a far greater purpose than to live your years here and be done. You exist to bring glory to God, and that is why you need to find your identity and purpose in Jesus. If something else is defining you, other than your relationship to Jesus, I encourage you to put it on the altar today. Surrender it to Jesus, and allow Him to either remove it altogether or to bring it back to life as something through which He can be glorified.

# MAKING AN ETERNAL IMPACT

*"Also He has put eternity in their hearts ..."*

ECCLESIASTES 3:11

Every four years, the world turns its attention to a sporting event that is like no other! The event lasts for weeks and involves athletes from all over the world. These athletes are not just competing for themselves, they are competing for their respective countries. Of course, I am talking about the Olympics. The pressure is intense and emotions run high, first because the whole world is watching, but also because a lifetime of dreams, hard work, and incredible sacrifice are either fulfilled or crushed in a moment's time.

Most Olympic athletes begin dreaming of competing at this level when they are still small children. Once their tremendous talent is noticed, the decision is made to sacrifice a lot of the normal experiences that most adolescents and teenagers go through in order to one day fulfill the dream of representing their country in the Olympic games.

## IT ALL COMES DOWN TO THIS

For those who are fortunate enough to make it to the games, and if they are lucky enough to make it to the final round, there is a critical moment prior to that final event when the thought arises—*everything I have trained for has come down to this moment: one race, one dive, one swim, one skate*. And for many of the athletes, there won't be a second opportunity. Imagine the pressure of having everything that you have ever hoped for and worked so hard to attain fall on one single event! That is a pressure most of us would not be able to carry, and it is one of the many reasons Olympians are so special.

The 2016 summer Olympic games took place in Rio de Janeiro, Brazil, and the U.S. sent divers David Boudia and Steele Johnson to compete in synchronized diving. They were considered strong medal contenders, and in the final round of the competition, they performed flawlessly and earned silver for the U.S.

Immediately after the second-place announcement, they were asked by NBC reporter Kelli Stavast: "What does it mean to come out here and medal in the synchro event?" I think David Boudia's response shocked a lot of people. He declared, "I just think the past week, there's just been an enormous amount of pressure, and I've felt it. You know, it's just an identity crisis. When my mind is on this, and I'm thinking I'm defined by this, then my mind goes crazy, but we both know our identity is in Christ. And we're just, we're thankful for this opportunity to be able to dive in front of Brazil, in front of the United States, and it's been an absolutely thrilling moment for us."

In that response, David Boudia hit on one of the most important and profound truths that every Christ follower needs to grasp—our identity is not found in what we do but in who we are in Christ. Boudia's diving partner, Steele Johnson, added this insight when he responded to a follow-up question: "I think the way David just described it was flawless. The fact that I was going into this event knowing that my identity is rooted in Christ and not what the result of this competition is just gave me peace. It gave me ease, and it let me enjoy the contest. It's cool because this is exciting, this is fun, but this is not what my identity will be for the rest of my life," he said. "Yeah, I'm Steele Johnson the Olympian, but at the same time, I'm here to love and serve Christ. My identity is rooted in Christ, not in the flips we're doing."

Realizing that your identity is found in who you are in Christ and not in what you do or in how you perform in a certain job, calling, or event is key to living a life of freedom and enjoyment, as well as having a life that will leave an eternal impact. Paul the apostle, in chapter 2 of the book of Ephesians, makes this point very clear when he declares: "*For we are His workmanship, created in Christ Jesus for good works, which God prepared beforehand that we should walk in them*" (verse 10).

## HIS WORKMANSHIP

The word *workmanship* is a very interesting word in the Greek. It's *poiēma*, from which we get our English word poem; but poem is not the primary meaning of this word. It's much broader and literally means "to make." So in first-century culture, the word came to speak of a work of art. It could be used in reference to a statue, a painting, a poem, or some sort of architecture. The word was most often used when people would reference a masterpiece.

We are God's masterpiece in the making. But it's important for us to understand that Paul isn't referring to what we are as human beings, or the human anatomy, even though it's true that God created us. The Bible declares in Psalm 139:14 that we are fearfully and wonderfully made, but Paul is speaking about something far greater and deeper; he's speaking in reference to redemption.

Notice he says that "*we are God's workmanship, created in Christ.*" We are not just created; the key phrase is "created in Christ." A sculptor can take a worthless piece of clay and fashion it into a beautiful statue worth over a million dollars. A painter can take a $3 piece of canvas, spread paint all over it, and create a beautiful painting that might sell for $300,000. A builder can take simple wood and fashion it into a house that can sell for millions of dollars. But only God can take a person who was lost, diseased by sin, broken, and selfish to the core, and make them into a saint. Only God can do that. Redemption, the fact that our sin and shame has been removed and placed upon Jesus, is what makes us His workmanship, His masterpiece; and each and every one of us has been created in Christ for an eternal purpose.

Paul makes it clear when he says that we are created in Christ Jesus "*for good works, which God prepared beforehand that we should walk in them.*" What are the "good works" we are to walk in? Well, think of it this way. A masterpiece is the deepest expression of the artist. It is defined as an artist's best piece of work. When you listen to a beautiful song, look at a stunning painting or a sculpture, or you read an inspiring poem, you are experiencing the deepest expression of its creator. It is their masterpiece.

## AN EXPRESSION OF THE ARTIST

What is absolutely fascinating to me about what Paul is saying is that the born-again believer is the Creator's deepest expression. So you are His art, His masterpiece. And what does He want to do with you? He wants to express Himself through your life.

The writer of the book of Hebrews says, "*In these last days God has spoken to us through His Son*" (Hebrews 1:2). God is still speaking today through His Son, as He lives His life out through the members that make up His church—His body, His bride. It's you in Christ and Christ in you on display for the world to see. God has made you unique; there is only one you, and Jesus wants to express Himself through that uniqueness.

An organist was alone one day in the church practicing a piece by Felix Mendelssohn, a famous German composer. After forty minutes of struggling through the song, he was so frustrated that he gathered up his music to leave, unaware that a stranger had walked into the church and was sitting in one of the back pews. As the organist turned to go, the stranger came forward and said, "Excuse me, do you mind if I play the piece?" The organist said, "No one ever touches this organ. Only me. I'm the only one that gets to play this." But after two more polite requests, the grumpy musician reluctantly gave him permission. The stranger sat down and filled the sanctuary with beautiful, flawless music. When he was finished, the stunned organist asked, "Who are you?" to which the man replied, "I'm Felix Mendelssohn."[8]

Just think about that. Here this man had almost prevented the song's creator from playing his own music. We can be guilty of the same thing. You see, there are times when we try to play the chords of our lives with little success, and yet we prevent the Creator from playing the beautiful music He has orchestrated for us. Like that stubborn organist, we are reluctant to take our hands off the keyboard and so sometimes God has to pry them off. But it's as we yield each aspect of our lives to His Spirit that He is able to move in us, working to mold and fashion us. What comes out is a beautiful song.

God has written a symphony for each one of us, and we need to give Him His rightful place as "conductor" in order for it to be heard. That's how the masterpiece is created. His Spirit in our hearts is always seeking to remind us that the Lord has us here for a reason that goes far beyond our own personal pleasure and enjoyment. The music of our lives is being written for the world to hear and for God's own pleasure and glory.

## WITH / IN / UPON

A few days before His death, Jesus had a conversation with His disciples about the Holy Spirit. He tells them in John 14:17 that the Holy Spirit was *with* them, but there was coming a day when He would be living *in* them. The Bible tells us that the Holy Spirit is the one who draws people to Jesus and convicts the world of sin and righteousness. Once a person puts their faith in Jesus Christ, believing that He died on the cross to pay the price for their sins and rose again in order to give them life, the Holy Spirit takes up residence in their hearts and begins that process of teaching, guiding, and transforming their lives. The theological term is sanctification—the process of being transformed and set apart for God.

John 20:21 describes the day that the apostles were indwelt with the Holy Spirit. It happened after the resurrection. The apostles were meeting together in an undisclosed residence when Jesus suddenly appeared to them in the room. They were startled to see Him, and He responded by saying, *"Be not afraid."* Jesus then breathed on them and said, "Receive the Holy Spirit." In that moment, the apostles were indwelt with the Holy Spirit. But that was just the beginning of this new relationship.

In Acts chapter 1 we read of another meeting that took place between Jesus and His disciples, prior to His ascension into heaven, where Jesus told them to go into Jerusalem and wait for the Holy Spirit to *come upon* them. So Jesus clearly makes three distinctions concerning their relationship with the Holy Spirit:

- The Holy Spirit was *with* them
- The Holy Spirit would be *in* them
- The Holy Spirit would come *upon* them

Jesus went on to promise His disciples that when the Holy Spirit came upon them, they would be empowered by Him to be His witnesses. Jesus referred to this as being *baptized in the Holy Spirit.*

Acts chapter 1, verses 4 through 8, records Luke's account of the conversation:

*And being assembled together with them, He commanded them not to depart from Jerusalem, but to wait for the Promise of the Father, "which," He said, "you have heard from Me; for John truly baptized with water, but you shall be baptized with the Holy Spirit not many days from now." Therefore, when they had come to-*

*gether, they asked Him, saying, "Lord, will You at this time restore the kingdom to Israel?" And He said to them, "It is not for you to know times or seasons which the Father has put in His own authority. But you shall receive power when the Holy Spirit has come upon you; and you shall be witnesses to Me in Jerusalem, and in all Judea and Samaria, and to the end of the earth."*

## YOUR SPIRITUAL IDENTITY

Jesus was telling His disciples that He was empowering them to *be* His witnesses, not to go witnessing, mind you, but to be living, breathing expressions of who He was to a world that so desperately needed to know Him. Please don't miss this important reality: Jesus was calling His followers *then*, and He is calling us *now*, not to *do* something but to BE SOMETHING—to be His witnesses!

Listen, Christian, your identity is not to be found in doing. Your identity is to be found in being, realizing that you have been placed in Christ Jesus, covered in the blood of Christ. You have been set free from sin and shame, and you are free to live in an authentic, personal, and intimate daily relationship with Jesus. The Lord refers to you as His workmanship, His masterpiece in the making, and He wants you to believe that and to walk in it. His desire is for you to step into the moments that He places before you on a regular basis, moments that He preordained for you from the beginning of time, to "be Jesus" to someone who needs to see Him in a tangible way through your life.

Paul refers to Christ followers as ambassadors in 2 Corinthians 5:20. The role of an ambassador is to represent king and country in the foreign land to which they have been appointed. We are Christ's ambassadors in this world, and He declares it is not our home. The Holy Spirit is always ready to empower us to live for Jesus and represent Him in the individual spheres of influence where the Lord has placed us. This is what we would refer to as being *led by the Holy Spirit*, allowing Him to guide our daily lives in such a way that we become more kingdom minded. In chapter 9, we will explore in greater detail what this can look like in our day-to-day living and how the Lord wants to be glorified in the very ordinary aspects of our lives.

I think for some of you, this will be an eye-opening and freeing look at how easy it actually can be to make an eternal impact.

# GOD GLORIFIED IN THE ORDINARY

*"... for thou hast created all things, and for thy pleasure they are and were created."*

REVELATION 4:11 KJV

One of my all-time favorite missionary biographies is *Bruchko*. This book tells the story of Bruce Olson, a nineteen-year-old young man who bought a one-way ticket to South America. He traveled into the uncharted jungles of northeast Colombia, where he found the Motilones, a fierce, primitive Indian tribe. Though Olson had no official sponsorship from a mission's board or organization, he has lived with the Indians since 1961, leading countless numbers of them to faith in Jesus Christ. God also has used him to establish medical clinics and schools for the tribe. He has translated

Scripture into their language, won the friendship of four presidents of Colombia, and has made appearances before the United Nations because of his efforts.

*Bruchko* is one of those inspiring stories that reminds us of what God can do with a life that is fully surrendered to Him. Bruce's life inspires us to attempt "great things" for God and to believe in a big God, with whom nothing is impossible.

For many of us, the thought of making a great eternal impact for God brings to mind stories like *Bruchko*. Or perhaps we envision an evangelist who preaches at the crusades where thousands give their lives to Christ. Some might even picture a wealthy person who is able to give a million dollars to the cause of Christ. And in this day and age, where social media is so prevalent, it is those types of people and stories that are often highlighted.

We hear pastors seeking to inspire their listeners to dream big, to believe that the Lord can use their lives to do great things. As a pastor myself, I understand that practice, for the Bible is filled with accounts of God using ordinary people to do extraordinary things. So I am a believer in dreaming big and in encouraging people to step out in faith when God calls. But sometimes, I think our definition of what constitutes a great thing in God's eyes is a bit skewed.

EXTRAORDINARY OR EXTRA ORDINARY?

The truth of the matter is that very few of you who are reading this book will be called to leave your homeland and go to a foreign country as a missionary. And even if you are, the probability of you being used by God to lead an entire village or town to Christ is not likely to happen. Those stories are few and far between and have less to do with the missionary and more to do with the sovereignty of Almighty God. I know many wonderful missionaries who have spent years faithfully ministering to a small group of people with little or no recognition from anyone. They serve because they love Jesus; they serve because they love the people they have been called to minister to; they serve because God called them to go and they went. There will be no books written about them, their stories will be largely untold, and they will never know the full impact of their sacrifice until they stand before the Lord in His glory.

Likewise, there are very few people who are called to be world-renowned evangelists who pack out stadiums, and there certainly aren't many Christians with the resources to give a million dollars to the cause of Christ!

## AN ETERNAL IMPACT IN THE ORDINARY

So what does this mean for the average person—the man or woman who is working forty to sixty hours per week? How can he or she make an eternal impact? What does it mean for the mom whose life revolves around taking care of her kids—running them to school and sports, helping with homework, and volunteering at school functions? Can she make an eternal impact? Or what about the student plugging away at college, whose life is consumed with studies and tests and the daily grind who feels like it's never going to end? Do they have to put this idea of making an eternal impact on hold until their education is finished and their career has begun?

The obvious answer is an emphatic *No!* Every single believer in Jesus Christ is His workmanship and has been created *"for good works, which God prepared beforehand that we should walk in them"* (Ephesians 2:10). God has a mission, and He has enlisted all of us to be a part of it; we just need to discover the role God wants us to play in this particular season of our lives. We are all God's servants, and He is simply looking for us to be faithful (1 Corinthians 4:2).

MISSION POSSIBLE

*Mission Impossible* was another television show we watched as a family while I was growing up. (For all my younger readers, yes, *Mission Impossible* was a weekly TV show long before Tom Cruise turned it into a popular movie series.) The show typically began in the same way: the leader of the team, Jim Phelps (played by actor Peter Graves), would listen to a tape recording that outlined the team's next mission. The end of the message would include this phrase: "Your mission, Jim, should you choose to accept it ..." And Jim and the team always accepted. But that was a TV show; what about real life? Well, God has a mission that He has selected for each one of us, and He is waiting to see if we are going to accept it.

The problem that many believers experience is they spend countless days, weeks, and sometimes even years trying to figure out what their mission is, when in reality, the mission God has chosen for each person is plainly seen in the pages of Scripture. It is the same mission that God gave to the first two human beings, Adam and Eve, and it's found in the first book of the Bible. In Genesis 1:27–28, we are told, *"So God created man in His own image; in the image of God He created him; male and female He created them. Then God blessed them, and God said to them, 'Be fruitful and multiply; fill the earth and subdue it; have dominion over the fish of the sea, over the birds of the air, and over every living thing that moves on the earth."'*

Verse 27 speaks of our unique calling to be image bearers of God. Mankind was made in His image, with a moral compass, and created to live in relationships, first with God, then with others. Verse 28 is the key to the mission. Notice how it starts, *"Then God blessed them,"* meaning the mission that God gave to man was meant to be a blessing and not a burden. There is something really valuable for us to grab a hold of in that truth—fulfilling God's mission for our lives is meant to bring blessing rather than adding a burden. *But what is the mission,* you ask? Look again at what the Lord said next in verse 28: *"Be fruitful and multiply; fill the earth and subdue it; have dominion over the fish of the sea, over the birds of the air, and over every living thing that moves on the earth."*

We can summarize the mission that God gave to Adam and Eve in this simple way. They were to:

- Love God and love each other (be fruitful and multiply).
- Take care of what God had placed into their hands.

That was it! And God has given that same mission to each and every one of us. We are to love God with everything in us—heart, soul, mind, and strength—be fruitful and multiply (physically and spiritually), and take care of what He has placed into our hands. This is how we make an eternal impact in the ordinary aspects of our lives. The question for consideration now is what has God placed into your hands?

## TIME IS IN YOUR HANDS

One of the greatest commodities we have to offer to God is our time. But the question is, how do we use it? Let's say you sleep eight hours a day and you live to be eighty years old. That equates to 467,200 waking hours in your lifetime to make an impact. Now, you could argue that a large period of your waking life is spent at work, but work is one of the places where Jesus has given you a sphere of influence. So even if we deduct the working hours, we still have over 233,600 waking hours entrusted to us by God. Imagine the eternal impact for the glory of God if you were more intentional about the use of your time. After all, intentional living is something God calls us to do. Psalm 90:12 states; *"Teach us to number our days, that we may gain a heart of wisdom."* Intentional living is about understanding why you do what you do and why you don't do what you don't do.

Being intentional with your time is discerning the difference between simply being busy and being productive. You can easily fall into the rut of busyness when you are constantly responding to the most urgent needs around you. But being productive is an awareness of what you are called to do and creating habits and rhythms that will help you accomplish those things. Being intentional about your time means that you will say "no" to things that distract you and pull you away from your mission.

## CHILDREN ARE IN OUR HANDS

Being a parent, whether through natural childbirth or adoption, is one of the greatest privileges that God gives to His people. And for many of us, our most significant eternal impact will be *someone* we raise rather than *something* we do.

All of you mothers out there who work so hard every day to take care of your home and tend to the needs of your family, please don't view what you do as mundane or unimportant in the big scheme of things. On the contrary, those tasks are exactly what the Lord has put into your hands. Your commitment and diligence to make your home a safe and loving place for your family to dwell in, where the name of Jesus is praised and the principles of the Gospel are seen, will help your children live as Christ followers in their sphere of influence. I heard of one mother who hung a plaque next to her kitchen sink that read

"Divine service happens here three times a day." That is a great attitude to have. What has the Lord put into your hands? What resources, opportunities, or people has He placed within your sphere of influence to have an impact upon? I guarantee that our kids are at the top of that list!

Parents need to learn to be intentional, looking for opportunities to bring Jesus into the conversations and daily routines of life with their kids. In the book of Deuteronomy, the Lord instructed the people of Israel in this way, *"Hear, O Israel: The LORD our God, the LORD is one! You shall love the LORD your God with all your heart, with all your soul, and with all your strength"* (Deuteronomy 6:4–5). As parents, we need to be purposeful in cultivating a love for God in the hearts of our children. At the end of the day, our primary goal is for our kids to love the Lord with all of their hearts.

The following verse gives insight into what this should look like practically:

> *And these words which I command you today shall be in your heart. You shall teach them diligently to your children, and shall talk of them when you sit in your house, when you walk by the way, when you lie down, and when you rise up. You shall bind them as a sign on your hand,*

*and they shall be as frontlets between your eyes.*
*You shall write them on the doorposts of your*
*house and on your gates.*

—Deuteronomy 6:6–9

As we see in the above passage, we are to be daily looking for those moments and opportunities to reveal Jesus to our children. In the Christian culture, we can have the tendency to separate things into two categories—the sacred and the secular. Consequently, Christian kids grow up compartmentalizing their lives. The principle of Deuteronomy 6 is to make every situation a sacred one, and we can do that by bringing the Lord into the conversation.

In other words, as you walk by the way, direct their attention to those things around you that speak of the creative genius of God—a flower, the form of a cloud, or the shape of a mountain. The more you do that, the more your children will grow up appreciating and respecting the artistic side of God.

When you sit down for dinner with your family, talk to your children about their day; ask them about their troubles. Maybe there's a conflict with a friend, or they're worried about tomorrow's test. Then, take that opportunity to immediately pray for them. In doing so, your kids will learn what it means to cast all their cares upon God because He cares for them (1 Peter 5:7).

Listen, you might not be able to have structured family devotions every day with your kids. You will find that the older they get, the harder that becomes because of their hectic schedules, with school, games, practices, and church functions. But you can have teachable moments throughout the day as you drive in the car, as you sit down for breakfast, when they are texting you about something going on, or even when they are fighting with their siblings. If you are intentional about the mission, you will seize those moments to bring God into their daily living. In this way, they will learn about the heart of God for them, and for those around them, and they will also learn to love God with all their heart, soul, mind, and strength.

If parents live with the big picture in mind—the realization that we exist on planet earth to bring God glory and to be a part of His mission to bring lost people into a relationship with His Son—that will have a contagious effect upon our kids. And when you send your kids off to school, college, or into the workforce, they will have a greater awareness of this important truth: their life is not their own, they exist for Jesus. By setting an example, your children will be more likely to use their gifts, talents, and calling in the field or profession that they choose, to glorify God and impact their sphere of influence.

So I will say it again, your biggest impact for God might not be in something that you do, but in someone that you raise.

## MAKING AN IMPACT WITH YOUR BUSINESS

If you are a business owner, God has placed into your hands a tool through which you have the opportunity to be a faithful example of Christ. How? By being a man or woman of integrity. You have the responsibility of treating clients and coworkers respectfully, remembering that they are all people who have been created in the image of God. He loves them, and Jesus died that they may be saved. You can reflect the heart of God by being more interested in people rather than the bottom line. In a world where cutthroat business is so often the norm, you can emulate Christ by being a servant leader to those who work for you. I would encourage you to adopt this mentality—that your place of business might not be the last place your employee works, but it will be remembered as the best place they ever worked.

In order to do that, you need to continually remind yourself that you are His workmanship, and you get to be the expression of our artistic God to those who come across your path. And consider this: maybe God wants to use your company, not only to enable you to make a comfortable living and employ others, but to make an impact on the needy in the world in the name of Christ.

Rick and Melissa Hinnant are the founders of Grace and Lace, a company that specializes in lacey leg warmers. The company was doing well as a startup in 2011 with $800,000 in sales. The company is unique in that Melissa, who has a heart for India and spent some time in her teens traveling there for missions work, decided to donate a portion of the proceeds to help the people of India.

In 2012, the Hinnants made an appearance on the TV show, *Shark Tank*, and the investor, Barbara Corcoran, inspired by their designs and their vision, partnered with them financially. After their appearance on the show, the sales continued to grow, grossing $2.8 million in 2012. In 2013, Grace and Lace partnered with the humanitarian organization, Angel House, donating a portion of each sale to the effort of building orphanages in India. As of 2016, the company has grossed $19 million in sales, which has helped to open seven orphanages, rescuing hundreds of children off the streets and out of the slums. They are provided with shelter, a mattress, three meals a day, clean water, house parents, Bibles, and a private school education. In addition, they have opened a freedom home in Nepal that works to save women from human sex trafficking.

The Hinnants are a great example of an ordinary couple who realized they exist to make an eternal impact on this world. Imagine the impact your business might make for the cause of Christ! William Carey, also a lover of India and a missionary in the eighteenth century, said, "Expect great things from God; attempt great things for God."[9]

## GIFTS, TALENTS, AND ABILITIES

God has given us gifts and talents, and we are called to use them to the best of our ability, but for His glory, not our own. In Colossians 3:17, the apostle Paul put it this way: "*And **whatever** you do in word or deed, **do** all in the name of the Lord Jesus, giving thanks to God the Father through Him*" (emphasis mine). Paul also exhorts us in 1 Corinthians 10:31, "*Whatever you do, do all to the glory of God.*"

In the previous chapter, I mentioned Steele Johnson and David Boudia, the 2016 Olympic silver medalist divers. What many people don't know is that when Steele was younger, he was involved in a diving accident in which he almost lost his life. He obviously recovered and went on to compete very well at every level he participated in, finally earning a spot on the

2016 Olympic team. In an interview that was seen on national television, Steele professed, "God kept me alive, and He is still giving me the ability to do what I do. I'm Steele Johnson the Olympian, but at the same time, I'm here to love and serve Christ."[10]

One of my favorite quotes is from the film *Chariots of Fire*, a movie about Eric Liddel, the famed Olympic runner. In the film, Eric's sister is questioning his sacrifice to the sport, as she thinks that his time and efforts would be better suited to the mission field in China. She believed evangelism was Eric's ultimate calling in life and that he was wasting his time competing. I love his response, "God made me fast. And when I run, I feel His pleasure." Eric eventually did become a missionary, but he recognized his speed as a gift from God and gave Him the glory."[11]

How has God made you? What gifts and talents has He given you? Do you feel His pleasure when you use them? Revelation 4:11 exclaims, *"Thou art worthy, O Lord, to receive glory and honour and power: for thou hast created all things, and for thy pleasure they are and were created"* (KJV).

Are you naturally gifted as a mother? Do you feel God smiling down on you as you care for your children? You should! Are you gifted as a musician, able to skillfully play an instrument in a way that makes people smile, instead of making them cringe? Do you feel His pleasure as you play? You should! Are you naturally gifted in building and fixing things? Do you even realize that is a gift? Believe me, it is! I would love to naturally know how to build things and fix things, but it doesn't come easy. Thankfully, I have the You-Tube channel, which has helped me stumble through some fix-it endeavors with a mild degree of success, but some of you don't need a manual or a video. You have been uniquely designed by God to understand things on a mechanical level. I hope you thank God for that, for your gift has probably helped you to earn a living or save money. Is there someone in your sphere of influence that needs something fixed or built? If God has gifted you to do that, your act of kindness might be the very thing that opens the door for you to share a message of the love of Jesus with someone who desperately needs to hear it.

Our gifts are part of what God has placed into our hands. We can and should use those gifts and talents in a way that will bless others and make an eternal impact for the glory of God.

## TALENTS: USED OR BURIED?

In Matthew 25:14–30, Jesus tells the parable of the talents. In this parable, a master gave each of his three servants a bag of resources, according to their abilities.

The master then went on trip, and the servants were to use their resources while the master was away. The first two men took the talents and doubled them, and the master said to both of them upon his return: *"Well done, good and faithful servant; you have been faithful over a few things, I will make you ruler over many things. Enter into the joy of your lord"* (verse 23). He commended them for being faithful and rewarded them by putting more into their hands. However, the third servant in the story received a very harsh rebuke because he took the resources he had been given and simply buried them, not using them at all.

I have three questions for you as we close out this chapter:

- What has God placed into your hands?
- Are you using the resources, talents, and abilities that God has given you, or have you buried them, therefore robbing God, yourself, and others?
- Are you using your talents, abilities, and resources primarily on yourself, or are you using them to bless others?

God is looking for faithful servants who will use what He has placed into their hands to bless others and therefore make an eternal impact for His name and for

His glory! That is the mission. The question is, will we choose to accept it?

10

# PURPOSE IN
# THE PAIN

*"My bones are pierced in me at night, and my
gnawing pains take no rest."*

JOB 30:17

Several years ago, my wife and I were speaking at a
couple's retreat in another state, and we met a woman
I will call Mary. She was a vibrant woman whose life
radiated the love and joy of Jesus Christ. So I was really surprised to learn that Mary's past was filled with
many physical and emotional scars.

More about Mary's story in a minute, but I want
to note that there are similarities between the physical
and emotional scars we all carry. I have a scar above
the left side of my lip; it is not very noticeable, but it

is a reminder of a scary day in my life when a German shepherd police dog bit me. *How did that happen?* you ask. *Was it the result of a robbery attempt gone bad in your B.C. days?* No! It happened when I was four years old. The dog belonged to my neighbor friend, Frankie, and one day we were terrorizing his dog. Frankie was sticking a rake in the dog's face, and I was pulling the dog's tail (brilliant, right?). Yours truly lost that battle. It happened in a moment—the dog turned, and suddenly I had a hole in my face that required stitches and left a scar.

I have another scar on my leg, right above the knee, that was from a stab wound with a pencil. Eh? *A playground fight in grade school?* you ask. No; again, an accident. The pencil was in my friend's back pocket while we were playing basketball. I came down on him in just the right direction and got stabbed in the leg.

My biggest scar stretches across my backside and down my leg. This was the result of a major hip surgery I had while in my thirties. They plied me open like a tuna to put some titanium hardware in my body. That scar took a while to heal and is a very visible reminder of what I went through to be able to walk without pain.

The interesting thing about scars is that you really don't think about them until you see them in the mirror or someone asks you about them. Most of the time, scars don't even hurt, but they remind you of painful events. Everyone has a scar or two and a story to tell.

But even if some of you don't have any physical scars, most of you have emotional ones. Emotional scars take place when someone betrays our trust, stabs us in the back, or violates us in some way. These emotional scars can affect our lives in a far greater way than the physical ones. But there is a similarity in the process of how the scar is produced. A physical scar starts with a wound: the skin is punctured or torn, leaving a rawness that will often require stitches. In the early stages of the wound, it is sensitive, and when touched, a great deal of pain and discomfort is experienced. In order for the wound to heal, it needs time and tenderness. Oftentimes in the healing process, a scab will form, but a sudden brush against a wall or even the touch of someone's hand can reopen the wound, causing that initial pain to come searing back upon the nerve endings. But eventually the scab goes away and what is left is the scar, the reminder, of that eventful day when the wound occurred.

## EMOTIONAL SCARS

Emotional scars are similar. They start with a wound. They happen when someone hurts you so deeply that you are bleeding inside. Your heart is torn and aching, and just like with a physical scar, the healing process is going to involve time and tenderness. In the early stages, the wound is sensitive. If anything happens to you or is said that even remotely resembles the initial infliction, the pain in your heart emerges. Any reminder of that event is like peeling a scab—you begin bleeding all over again. With time, that wound will heal, but it will leave an emotional scar on your heart, the reminder that someone hurt you in a way that was far deeper than you could ever imagine.

## WILL IT DEFINE YOU?

The emotional scars that we have will affect us in one of two ways, depending on our perspective and our relationship with God. That scar will either be the thing that defines you as a victim, or it will be a symbol of the grace and faithfulness of God. It will serve as the constant reminder of the thing that ruined your life and shattered your dreams, or it will be a testimony to the ability of God to bring healing. Mary was a vivid example of this kind of grace and faithfulness. Her past did not define her; instead, she became a testimony to the healing power of God.

## THE SCAR OF ABUSE

We noticed Mary throughout the weekend, always laughing and engaged in conversation. She was a pretty woman in her late fifties, and there was a vibrancy and joy that seemed to pour out of her. From what we had observed, Mary was obviously a woman who knew that she was loved by God and by her husband; So, I was incredibly surprised when I heard her story.

Mary's first husband had been extremely abusive. He had claimed to be a Christian and regularly went to church but would often beat her. For years, Mary suffered in silence. There were times when she would show up to church with sunglasses on and wear them throughout the service to cover a black eye. On one occasion, the beating was so bad that her husband broke her leg. To make matters worse, when she finally got up the courage to tell her pastor, his response was appalling. He told her that if she would be a more submissive wife, those things wouldn't happen. In my opinion, a pastor who says such things has no business pretending to be a shepherd who is called to care for the flock of God.

Mary finally divorced her husband, but she lived with extreme anger and bitterness because of what she had been through. She even enrolled in self-defense and karate classes to learn how to protect herself. Mary told us that she would even provoke a confrontation with a man just to have an excuse to get into a fight so she could try to physically harm him. The emotional scars inflicted by her first husband had definitely defined her and left her bound in bitterness, anger, and hatred.

That began to change when she met her second husband, a godly man who, through tenderness and patience, helped her to heal and become whole. Mary was no longer defined by the abuse of her past. Instead, she now is able to identify herself as a daughter of God and is walking freely in the grace, forgiveness, and love of God, testifying to His power to heal and make whole again.

## PURPOSE IN THE PAIN

Over the years, I have heard many stories like Mary's—testimonies of people whose lives should have been ruined but were instead radically transformed by the healing power of God. The scar remains, but it stands as a symbol of God's power rather than a symbol of man's destruction. God wants to use our past hurts to reach the wounded people around us and share with them about the love and power of Jesus, who heals the brokenhearted and binds up their wounds (Psalm 147:3). We also have the opportunity to comfort others who are hurting with the comfort we have received from God. *"Blessed be the God and Father of our Lord Jesus Christ, the Father of mercies and God of all comfort, who comforts us in all our tribulation, that we might be able to comfort those who are in any trouble, with the comfort which we ourselves are comforted by God"* (2 Corinthians 1:3–4). Not only that, but when we move forward—past our pain—a transformation will take place and give us a testimony of God's glory and grace.

Author Warren Wiersbe writes in his book *Be Determined*, "God doesn't give us joy instead of sorrow, or joy in spite of sorrow, but joy in the midst of sorrow. It is not substitution but transformation."[12]

Jesus illustrated this truth vividly in speaking of a baby's birth: *"A woman, when she is in labor, has sorrow because her hour has come; but as soon as she has given birth to the child, she no longer remembers the anguish, for joy that a human being has been born into the world"* (John 16:21). The same baby that gives a mother pain also gives that mother joy! Her pain is not replaced by joy, but transformed into joy.

This principle is true in our lives as well. Painful circumstances often give birth to something beautiful and lasting. Think of the apostle Paul who called Timothy his true son in the faith (1 Timothy 1:2). Timothy was a joy in Paul's life, but do you remember where Paul found Timothy? It was in a town called Lystra, where an angry mob had brutally stoned Paul to death for sharing the Gospel, yet God miraculously brought him back to life! One of the most painful experiences that he had ever gone through was transformed into joy. The joy that was born out of that harrowing ordeal was the newfound relationship with this young man, Timothy. After witnessing Paul come back to life, Timothy became one of the apostle's most trusted and loyal companions. And later, when he needed a new pastor for his beloved church in Ephesus (his longest pastorate), Paul chose Timothy.

## STRENGTH IN WEAKNESS

Paul spoke of an ongoing affliction in his life, which he described as a thorn in the flesh, a messenger of Satan sent to buffet him (2 Corinthians 12:7). We are not sure if that thorn in the flesh was a person, a physical infirmity, or an actual demonic being, but Paul prayed constantly that the Lord would take it away. Finally, after one of his times of prayer, the Lord answered him with these words: *"My grace is sufficient for you, for My strength is made perfect in weakness"* (2 Corinthians 12:9a). Paul's response is recorded in verses 9 and 10: *"Therefore most gladly I will rather boast in my infirmities that the power of Christ may rest upon me. Therefore I take pleasure in infirmities, in reproaches, in needs, in persecutions, in distresses, for Christ's sake. For when I am weak, then I am strong."*

What Paul discovered that day is exactly what the Lord wants us to understand when it comes to the events in our lives that cause us to be marked by emotional scars. The scar is not going to go away; it will always be there, but it can be a symbol of the power of God to help us be overcomers rather than those who are overcome.

## THE WORLD PAYS ATTENTION TO OUR SUFFERINGS

I am personally convinced that people who do not yet know Jesus pay more attention to us in our difficulties than in our blessings. Those who are experiencing trouble in their lives take note when they see believers suffering well. What I mean by that is, when a Christian gets the promotion or wins the game, I don't think the unbeliever is impressed. In all honestly, I think they are annoyed that a "Christian" is being blessed when they are not. But do you know when they pay the most attention? I think it's when we don't get the promotion or when we get laid off of work or when our marriage blows up or when we lose the game. It is then that they perk up and pay attention. Why? Because they want to see the reality of our relationship with God in the midst of our struggles. When an unsaved person hears your story of pain, or hears about the wound that should have ruined your life but didn't because of your faith and relationship with God, that may be a life-changing turning point for them.

## EVIL TURNED TO GOOD

Joseph's life makes another powerful statement about God's purpose in pain. He suffered abuse at the hands of his brothers who ultimately sold him into slavery. But years later, when he finally saw them face-to-face, he said some amazing words: *"But as for you, you meant evil against me; but God meant it for good, in order to bring it about as it is this day, to save many people alive"* (Genesis 5:20). Though Joseph suffered for many years in Egypt, he witnessed the providence of God, who ultimately put him in a position of power and authority so he could save his family from famine!

What was true of Joseph is equally true for every believer—there is purpose in the pain. What Satan and others mean for evil, the Lord wants to use for good, that people around us might be eternally impacted through our scars. I believe the Holy Spirit residing in our hearts is constantly seeking to remind us of this reality. Our pain has a purpose, and through His grace and power, we can rise up and glorify Jesus in our weakness and suffering.

## THE FELLOWSHIP OF HIS SUFFERING

There is one more purpose for the pain that we endure and the scars that we obtain. Paul referred to it in Philippians 3:10 as *"the fellowship of [Christ's] suffering.*" Our Lord was scarred for our benefit, so when we go through times of being hurt by the ones we love, betrayed by people we thought we could trust, maligned by people who don't have all the facts, or even abused by those whose hearts are filled with hate, we enter into an exclusive club known as the fellowship of Christ's suffering. Those types of negative encounters that can leave our lives forever scarred give us a small taste of what Jesus endured on our behalf. And this really brings us back full circle to the beginning of this book. One of the main things that the Holy Spirit is seeking to do in our lives is to pull us deeper into intimacy with Jesus. I believe He uses our suffering and pain to do this. We are drawn into a better understanding of what Jesus endured for us, and we see more clearly how we are to respond to those who have hurt us. The painful, scarring moments of our lives are what the Lord is using to transform us into the image of His own dear Son (Romans 8:29).

I will end this final chapter with these wonderful words from the apostle Paul:

*What then shall we say to these things? If God is for us, who can be against us? He who did not spare His own Son, but delivered Him up for us all, how shall He not with Him also freely give us all things? Who shall bring a charge against God's elect? It is God who justifies. Who is he who con-*

*demns? It is Christ who died, and furthermore is also risen, who is even at the right hand of God, who also makes intercession for us. Who shall separate us from the love of Christ? Shall tribulation, or distress, or persecution, or famine, or nakedness, or peril, or sword? As it is written:*

*"For Your sake we are killed all day long; we are accounted as sheep for the slaughter."*

*Yet in all these things we are more than conquerors through Him who loved us. For I am persuaded that neither death nor life, nor angels nor principalities nor powers, nor things present nor things to come, nor height nor depth, nor any other created thing, shall be able to separate us from the love of God which is in Christ Jesus our Lord.*

—Romans 8:31–39

The Lord loves you, friend, and He is committed to completing the work that He has begun in you (Philippians 1:6). May His Spirit continually remind you of these truths: We have been redeemed to enjoy living in an intimate relationship with our Abba Father; life on this planet is the prologue to the real story of what we will be engaged in for Jesus here and now and for all eternity; and in the meantime, we can make an eternal impact on this world by living with the realization that God invites us to be a part of His mission. He is writing this ongoing story of redemption in the hearts of people all over the world, and it is our privilege to play a part in that story.

# CONCLUSION

I have lived in Southern California most of my life and have always resided no more than fifteen miles from the ocean. Consequently, I have spent countless hours at the beach and in the water. It's one of the things that has brought me a great deal of pleasure, whether catching waves in the surf, kayaking around the harbor, watching a beautiful sunset, or taking walks with my wife and our beloved dog, Reddington. I love being around the ocean.

Now, when you are swimming in the ocean, there is one thing you must always be mindful of—riptides. Sometimes riptides, or rip currents, are formidable; you can feel them pulling you out to sea or in a certain direction, left or right, as soon as you get into the water.

When the riptides are strong, it's almost easier to manage because you are mindful of them. But more often than not, rip currents are subtle. You can be swimming or floating in the ocean and not even realize you are being pulled out or pulled in a certain direction. It suddenly hits you when you look back at the shore and the people on it look like little dots because you have drifted so far. Or you search the shore for your group of friends and they are nowhere to be found. *Did they leave me*? *What happened*? It is then you realize that you have been in a subtle riptide, which has caused you to drift several hundred yards from the spot where you entered. One of the best ways to make sure you don't get swept out or swept down too far is to fix your eyes on something on the shore, like a lifeguard tower. That landmark becomes your true north, the point you keep coming back to. Without that focal point, you might end up in a place you don't want to be.

Life is also full of riptides, and sometimes they are very obvious. They are what I would call cultural riptides, and these occur when the climate and rhetoric of the culture scream in direct opposition to what is written in the pages of Scripture. But there are other more subtle currents in life that are less noticeable. They gradually pull on our hearts and challenge our priorities. Before we know it, we are spending too much time and energy pursuing things that are of no eternal value and will potentially hinder us from making any kind of eternal impact. We end up resembling the hamster on the wheel, exerting a ton of energy and time but going nowhere.

My prayer for you is that from this day forward, these three built-in longings of the Holy Spirit will serve as your true north. May you be able to distinguish the riptides of life from the gentle urgings of the Holy Spirit who is continuously pulling you in the direction of pursuing intimacy with God—the number one priority. May you hear the voice of the Spirit of God in your heart reminding you that this life is only the prologue to your story; the real story comes later—and involves what you will be doing with Jesus in His kingdom for all eternity. I pray you will remember that LATER IS LONGER! And I hope you will respond to the Holy Spirit's prompting—to make an eternal impact now—by living intentionally for Jesus in your sphere of influence and by taking care of what He has put into your hands. If you stay focused on your true north, you won't be sidetracked or swept away, and your life will be spiritually full and radically blessed.

# NOTES

---

[1]  https://www.scribd.com/document/314817259/Gato rade-Short-History.

[2]  Alexander Pope, "An Essay on Man." Poem published in 1733-1734.

[3]  Excerpted from "The Immutability of God," a sermon by Charles H. Spurgeon. Delivered on Sabbath Morning, January 7th, 1855, at New Park Street Chapel, Southwark.

[4]  Saint Augustine, *The Confessions (Book I)*.

[5]  Warren Wiersbe, *Too Soon to Quit*; Page 16, CLC Publications, March 1, 2010.

[6]  https://www.guideposts.org/comfort-hope/why-do-people-say-keep-your-fork.

[7]  Roy Jenkins, *Gladstone: A Biography* (New York, New York: Random House, 1997), 768 pages.

[8] http://www.preceptaustin.org/ephesians_sermon_illustrations_2.

[9] *The Baptist Magazine for 1830*. Vol. XXII. London: George Wightman, 1830, (July 1830):311.

[10] Steele Johnson – NBC Sports; August 2016.

[11] Hugh Hudson, et al. *Chariots of Fire*. Burbank, CA: Warner Home Video, 2005.

[12] Warren Wiersbe. *Be Determined (Nehemiah): Standing Firm in the Face of Opposition* (David C. Cook; June 1, 2009).